The Book of L

Mind and Body

by

Upton Sinclair

CHAPTER I

THE NATURE OF LIFE

(Attempts to show what we know about life; to set the bounds of real truth as distinguished from phrases and self-deception.)

If I could, I would begin this book by telling you what Life is. But unfortunately I do not know what Life is. The only consolation I can find is in the fact that nobody else knows either.

We ask the churches, and they tell us that male and female created He them, and put them in the Garden of Eden, and they would have been happy had not Satan tempted them. But then you ask, who made Satan, and the explanation grows vague. You ask, if God made Satan, and knew what Satan was going to do, is it not the same as if God did it himself? So this explanation of the origin of evil gets you no further than the Hindoo picture of the world resting on the back of a tortoise, and the tortoise on the head of a snake—and nothing said as to what the snake rests on.

Let us go to the scientist. I know a certain physiologist, perhaps the greatest in the world, and his eager face rises before me, and I hear his quick, impetuous voice declaring that he knows what Life is; he has told it in several big volumes, and all I have to do is to read them. Life is a tropism, caused by the presence of certain combinations of chemicals; my friend knows this, because he has produced the thing in his test-tubes. He is an exponent of a way of thought called Monism, which finds the ultimate source of being in forms of energy manifesting themselves as matter; he shows how all living things arise from that and sink back into it.

But question this scientist more closely. What is this "matter" that you are so sure of? How do you know it? Obviously, through sensations. You never know matter itself, you only know its effects upon you, and you assume that the matter must be there to cause the sensation. In other words, "matter," which seems so real, turns out to be merely "a permanent possibility of sensation." And suppose there were to be sensations, caused, for example, by a sportive demon who liked to make fun of eminent physiologists—then there might be the appearance of matter and nothing else; in other words, there might be mind, and various states of mind. So we discover that the materialist, in the philosophic sense, is making just as large an act of faith, is pronouncing just as bold a dogma as any priest of any religion.

This is an old-time topic of disputation. Before Mother Eddy there was Bishop Berkeley, and before Berkeley, there was Plato, and they and the materialists disputed until their hearers cried in despair, "What is Mind? No matter! What is Matter? Never mind!" But a century or two ago in a town of Prussia there lived a little, dried-up professor of philosophy, who sat himself down in his room and fixed his eyes on a church steeple outside the window, and for years on end devoted himself to examining the tools of thought with which the human mind is provided, and deciding just what work and how much of it they are fitted to do. So came the proof that our minds are incapable of reaching to or dealing with any ultimate reality whatever, but can comprehend only phenomena—that is to say, appearances —and their relations one with another. The Koenigsberg professor proved this once for all time, setting forth four propositions about ultimate reality, and proving them by exact and irrefutable logic, and then proving by equally exact and irrefutable logic their precise opposites and contraries. Anybody who has read and comprehended the four "antinomies" of Immanuel Kant[A] knows that metaphysics is as dead a subject as astrology, and that all the complicated theories which the philosophers from Heraclitus to Arthur Balfour have spun like spiders out of their inner consciousness, have no more relation to reality than the intricacies of the game of chess.

[A]   See Paulsen: "Life of Kant."

The writer is sorry to make this statement, because he spent a lot of time reading these philosophers and acquainting himself with their subtle theories. He learned a whole language of long words, and even the special meanings which each philosopher or school of philosophers give to them. When he had got through, he had learned, so far as metaphysics is concerned, absolutely nothing, and had merely the job of clearing out of his mind great masses of verbal cobwebs. It was not even good intellectual training; the metaphysical method of thought is a *trap*. The person who thinks in absolutes and ultimates is led to believe that he has come to conclusions about reality, when as a matter of fact he has merely proved what he wants to believe; if he had wanted to believe the opposite, he could have proven that exactly as well—as his opponents will at once demonstrate.

If you multiply two feet by two feet, the result represents a plain surface, or figure of two dimensions. If you multiply two feet by two feet by two feet, you have a solid, or figure of three dimensions—such as the world in which we live and move. But now, suppose you multiply two feet by two feet by two feet by two feet, what does that represent? For ages the minds of mathematicians and philosophers have been tempted by this fascinating problem of the "fourth dimension." They have worked out by analogy what such a world would be like. If you went into this "fourth dimension," you could turn yourself inside out, and come back to our present world in that condition, and no one of your three-dimension friends would be able to imagine how you had managed it, or to put you back again the way you belonged. And in this, it seems to me, we have the perfect analogy of metaphysical thinking. It is the "fourth dimension" of the mind, and plays as much havoc with sound thinking as a physical "fourth dimension" would play with—say, the prison system. A man who takes up an absolute—God, immortality, the origin of being, a first cause, free will, absolute right or wrong, infinite time or space, final truth, original substance, the "thing in itself"—that man disappears into a fourth dimension, and turns himself inside out or upside down or hindside foremost, and comes back and exhibits himself in triumph; then, when he is ready, he effects another disappearance, and another change, and is back on earth an ordinary human being.

The world is full of schools of thought, theologians and metaphysicians and professors of academic philosophy, transcendentalists and theosophists and Christian Scientists, who perform such mental monkey-shines continuously before our eyes. They prove what they please, and the fact that no two of them prove the same thing makes clear to us in the end that none of them has proved anything. The Christian Scientist asserts that there is no such thing as matter, but that pain is merely a delusion of mortal mind; he continues serene in this faith until he runs into an automobile and sustains a compound fracture of the femur—whereupon he does exactly what any of the rest of us do, goes to a competent surgeon and has the bone set. On the other hand, some devoted young Socialists of my acquaintance have read Haeckel and Dietzgen, and adopted the dogma that matter is the first cause, and that all things have grown out of it and return to it; they have seen that the brain decays after death, they declare that the soul is a function of the brain—and because of such theories they deliberately reject the most powerful modes of appeal whereby men can be swayed to faith in human solidarity.

The best books I know for the sweeping out of metaphysical cobwebs are "The Philosophy of Common Sense" and "The Creed of a Layman," by Frederic Harrison, leader of the English Positivists, a school of thought established by Auguste Comte. But even as I recommend these books, I recall the dissatisfaction with which I left them; for it appears that the Positivists have their dogmas like all the rest. Mr. Harrison is not content to say that mankind has not the mental tools for dealing with ultimate realities; he must needs prove that mankind never will and never can have these tools, I look back upon the long process of evolution and ask myself, What would an oyster think about Positivism? What would be the opinion of, let us say, a young turnip on the subject of Mr. Frederic Harrison's thesis? It may well be that the difference between a turnip and Mr. Harrison is not so great as will be the difference between Mr. Harrison and that super-race which some day takes possession of the earth and of all the universe. It does not seem to me good science or good sense to dogmatize about what this race will know, or what will be its tools of thought. What does seem to me good science and good sense is to take the tools which we now possess and use them to their utmost capacity.

What is it that we know about life? We know a seemingly endless stream of sensations which manifest themselves in certain ways, and seem to inhere in what we call things and beings. We observe incessant change in all these phenomena, and we examine these changes and discover their ways. The ways seem to be invariable; so completely so that for practical purposes we assume them to be invariable, and base all our calculations and actions upon this assumption. Manifestly, we could not live otherwise, and the spread of scientific knowledge is the further tracing out of such "laws"—that is to say, the ways of behaving of existence—and the extending of our belief in their invariability to wider and wider fields.

Once upon a time we were told that "the wind bloweth where it listeth." But now we are quite certain that there are causes for the blowing of the wind, and when our researches have been carried far enough, we shall be able to account for and to predict every smallest breath of air. Once we were told that dreams came from a supernatural world; but now we are beginning to analyze dreams, and to explain what they come from and what they mean. Perhaps we still find human nature a bewildering and unaccountable thing; but some day we shall know enough of man's body and his mind, his past and his present, to be able to explain human nature and to produce it at will, precisely as today we produce certain reactions in our test-tubes, and do it so invariably that the most cautious financier will invest tens of millions of dollars in a process, and never once reflect that he is putting too much trust in the permanence of nature.

In many departments of thought great specialists are now working, experimenting and observing by the methods of science. If in the course of this book we speak of "certainty," we mean, of course, not the "absolute" certainty of any metaphysical dogma, but the practical certainty of everyday common sense; the certainty we feel that eating food will satisfy our hunger, and that tomorrow, as today, two and two will continue to make four.

CHAPTER II

THE NATURE OF FAITH

(Attempts to show what we can prove by our reason, and what we know intuitively; what is implied in the process of thinking, and without which no thought could be.)

The primary fact that we know about life is growth. Herbert Spencer has defined this growth, or evolution, in a string of long words which may be summed up to mean: the process whereby a number of things which are simple and like one another become different parts of one thing which is complex. If we observe this process in ourselves, and the symptoms of it in others, we discover that when it is proceeding successfully, it is accompanied by a sensation of satisfaction which we call happiness or pleasure; also that when it is thwarted or repressed, it is accompanied by a different sensation which we call pain. Subtle metaphysicians, both inside the churches and out, have set themselves to the task of proving that there must be some other object of life than the continuance of these sensations of pleasure which accompany successful growth. They have proven to their own satisfaction that morality will collapse and human progress come to an end unless we can find some other motive, something more permanent and more stimulating, something "higher," as they phrase it. All I can say is that I gave reverent attention to the arguments of these moralists and theologians, and that for many years I believed their doctrines; but I believe them no longer.

I interpret the purpose of life to be the continuous unfoldment of its powers, its growth into higher forms—that is to say, forms more complex and subtly contrived, capable of more intense and enduring kinds of that satisfaction which is nature's warrant of life. If you wish to take up this statement and argue about it, please wait until you have read the chapter "Nature and Man," and noted my distinction between instinctive life and rational life. For men, the word "growth" does not mean *any* growth, *all* growth, blind and indiscriminate growth. It does not mean growth for the tubercle bacillus, nor growth for the anopheles mosquito, nor growth for the house-fly, the spider and the louse. Neither do we mean that the purpose of man's own life is *any* pleasure, *all* pleasure, blind and indiscriminate pleasure; the pleasure of alcohol, the pleasure of cannibalism, the pleasure of the modern form of cannibalism which we call "making money." We have survived in the struggle for existence by the cooperative and social use of our powers of judgment; and our judgment is that which selects among forms of growth, which gives preference to wheat and corn over weeds, and to self-control and honesty over treachery and greed.

So when we say that the purpose of life is happiness, we do not mean to turn mankind loose at a hog-trough; we mean that our duty as thinkers is to watch life, to test it, to pick and choose among the many forms it offers, and to say: This kind of growth is more permanent and full of promise, it is more fertile, more deeply satisfactory; therefore, we choose this, and sanction the kind of pleasure which it brings. Other kinds we decide are temporary and delusive; therefore we put in jail anyone who sells alcoholic drink, and we refuse to invite to our home people who are lewd, and some day we shall not permit our children to attend moving picture shows in which the modern form of cannibalism is glorified.

The reader, no doubt, has been taught a distinction between "science" and "faith." He is saying now, "You believe that everything is to be determined by human reason? You reject all faith?" I answer, No; I am not rejecting faith; I am merely refusing to apply it to objects with which it has nothing to do. You do not take it as a matter of faith that a package of sugar weighs a pound; you put it on the scales and find out—in other words, you make it a matter of experiment. But all the creeds of all the religious sects are full of pronouncements which are no more matters of faith than the question of the weighing of sugar. Is pork a wholesome article of food or is it not? All Christians will readily acknowledge that this is a matter to be determined by the microscope and other devices of experimental science; but then some Jew rises in the meeting and puts the question: Is dancing injurious to the character? And immediately all members of the Methodist Episcopal Church vote to close the discussion.

What is faith? Faith is the instinct which underlies all being, assuring us that life is worth while and honest, a thing to be trusted; in other words, it is the certainty that successful growth always is and always will be accompanied by pleasure. The most skeptical scientist in the world, even my friend the physiologist who proves that life is nothing but a tropism, and can be produced by mixing chemicals in test-tubes—this eager friend is one of the most faithful men I know. He is burning up with the faith that knowledge is worth possessing, and also that it is possible of attainment. With what boundless scorn would he receive any suggestion to the contrary —for example, the idea that life might be a series of sensations which some sportive demon is producing for the torment of man! More than that, this friend is burning up with the certainty that knowledge can be spread, that his fellow men will receive it and apply it, and that it will make them happy when they do. Why else does he write his learned books in defense of the materialist philosophy?

And that same faith which animates the great monist animates likewise every child who toddles off to school, and every chicken which emerges from an egg, and every blade of grass which thrusts its head above the ground. Not every chicken survives, of course, and all the blades of grass wither in the fall; nevertheless, the seeds of grass are spread, and chickens make food for philosophers, and the great process of life continues to manifest its faith. In the end the life process produces man, who, as we shall presently see, takes it up, and judges it, and makes it over to suit himself.

You will note from this that I am what is called an optimist; whereas some of the great philosophers of the world have called themselves pessimists. But I notice with a smile that these are often the men who work hardest of all to spread their ideas, and thus testify to the worthwhileness of truth and the perfectibility of mankind. There has come to be a saying among settlement workers and physicians, who are familiar with poverty and its effects upon life, that there are no bad babies and good babies, there are only sick babies and well babies. In the same way, I would say there are no pessimists and optimists, there are only mentally sick people and mentally well people. Everywhere throughout life, both animal and vegetable, health means happiness, and gives abundant evidence of that fact. All healthy life is satisfactory to itself; when it develops reason, it tries to find out why, and this is yet another testimony to the fact that having power and using it is pleasant. When I was in college the professor would propound the old question: "Would you rather be a happy pig or an unhappy philosopher?" My answer always was: "I would rather be a happy philosopher." The professor replied: "Perhaps that is not possible." But I said: "I will prove that it is!"

CHAPTER III

THE USE OF REASON

(Attempts to show that in the field to which reason applies we are compelled to use it, and are justified in trusting it.)

The great majority of people are brought up to believe that some particular set of dogmas are objects of faith, and that there are penalties more or less severe for the application of reason to these dogmas. What particular set it happens to be is a matter of geography; in a crowded modern city like New York, it is a matter of the particular block on which the child is born. A child born on Hester Street will be taught that his welfare depends upon his never eating meat and butter from the same dish. A child born on Tenth Avenue will be taught that it is a matter of his not eating meat on Fridays. A child born on Madison Avenue will be taught that it is a question of the precise metaphysical process by which bread is changed into human body and wine into human blood. Each of these children will be assured that his human reason is fallible, that it is extremely dangerous to apply it to this "sacred" subject, and that the proper thing to do is to accept the authority of some ancient tradition, or some institution, or some official, or some book for which a special sanction is claimed.

Has there ever been in the world any revelation, outside of or above human reason? Could there ever be such a thing? In order to test this possibility, select for yourself the most convincing way by which a special revelation could be handed down to mankind. Take any of the ancient orthodox ways, the finding of graven tablets on a mountain-top, or a voice speaking from a burning bush, or an angel appearing before a great concourse of people and handing out a written scroll. Suppose that were to happen, let us say, at the next Yale-Harvard football game; suppose the news were to be flashed to the ends of the earth that God had thus presented to mankind an entirely new religion. What would be the process by which the people of London or Calcutta would decide upon that revelation? First, they would have to consider the question whether it was an American newspaper fake—by no means an easy question. Second, they would have to consider the chances of its being an optical delusion. Then, assuming they accepted the sworn testimony of ten thousand mature and competent witnesses, they would have to consider the possibility of someone having invented a new kind of invisible aeroplane. Assuming they were convinced that it was really a supernatural being, they would next have to decide the chances of its being a visitor from Mars, or from the fourth dimension of space, or from the devil. In considering all this, they would necessarily have to examine the alleged revelation. What was the literary quality of it? What was the moral quality of it? What would be the effect upon mankind if the alleged revelation were to be universally adopted and applied?

Manifestly, all these are questions for the human reason, the human judgment; there is no other method of determining them, there would be nothing for any individual person, or for men as a whole to do, except to apply their best powers, and, as the phrase is, "make up their minds" about the matter. Reason would be the judge, and the new revelation would be the prisoner at the bar. Humanity might say, this is a real inspiration, we will submit ourselves to it and follow it, and allow no one from now on to question it. But inevitably there would be some who would say, "Tommyrot!" There would be others who would say, "This new revelation isn't working, it is repressing progress, it is stifling the mind." These people would stand up for their conviction, they would become martyrs, and all the world would have to discuss them. And who would decide between them and the great mass of men? Reason, the judge, would decide.

It is perfectly true that human reason is fallible. Infallibility is an absolute, a concept of the mind, and not a reality. Life has not given us infallibility, any more than it has given us omniscience, or omnipotence, or any other of those attributes which we call divine. Life has given us powers, more or less weak, more or less strong, but all capable of improvement and development. Reason is the tool whereby mankind has won supremacy over the rest of the animal kingdom, and is gradually taking control of the forces of nature. It is the best tool we have, and because it is the best, we are driven irresistibly to use it. And how strange that some of us can find no better use for it than to destroy its own self! Visit one of the Jesuit fathers and hear him seek to persuade you that reason is powerless against faith and must abdicate to faith. You answer, "Yes, father, you have persuaded me. I admit the fallibility of my mortal powers; and I begin by applying my doubts of them to the arguments by which you have just convinced me. I was convinced, but of course I cannot be sure of a conviction, attained by fallible reason. Therefore I am just where I was before—except that I am no longer in position to be certain of anything."

You answer in good faith, and take up your hat and depart, closing the door of the good father's study behind you. But stop a moment, why do you close the door? You close the door because your reason tells you that otherwise the cold air outside will blow in and make the good father uncomfortable. You put your hat on, because your reason has not yet been applied to the problem of the cause of baldness. You step out onto the street, and when you hear a sudden noise, you step back onto the curbstone, because your reason tells you that an automobile is coming, and that on the sidewalk you are safe from it. So you go on, using your reason in a million acts of your life whereby your life is preserved and developed. And if anybody suggested that the fallibility of your reason should cause you to delay in front of an automobile, you would apply your reason to the problem of that person and decide that he was insane. And I say that just as there is insanity in everyday judgments and relationships, so there is insanity in philosophy, metaphysics and religion; the seed and source of all this kind of insanity being the notion that it is the duty of anybody to believe anything which cannot completely justify itself as reasonable.

Nowadays, as ideas are spreading, the champions of dogma are hard put to it, and you will find their minds a muddle of two points of view. The Jewish rabbi will strive desperately to think of some hygienic objection to the presence of meat and butter on the same plate; the Catholic priest will tell you that fish is a very wholesome article of food, and that anyhow we all eat too much; the Methodist and the Baptist and the Presbyterian will tell you that if men did not rest one day in seven their health would break down. Thus they justify faith by reason, and reconcile the conflict between science and theology. Accepting this method, I experiment and learn that it improves my digestion and adds to my working power if I play tennis on Sunday. I follow this indisputably rational form of conduct—and find myself in conflict with the "faith" of the ancient State of Delaware, which obliges me to serve a term in its state's prison for having innocently and unwittingly desecrated its day of holiness!

If you read Professor Bury's little book, "A History of Freedom of Thought," you will discover that there has been a long conflict over the right of men to use their minds—and the victory is not yet. The term "free thinker," which ought to be the highest badge a man could wear, is still almost everywhere throughout America a term of vague terror. In the State of California today there is a Criminal Syndicalism Act, which provides a maximum of fourteen years in jail for any person who shall write or publish or speak any words expressive of the idea that the United States government should be overthrown in the same way that it was established—that is, by force; only a few months ago the writer of this book was on the witness stand for two days, and had the painful, almost incredible experience of being battered and knocked about by an inquisitive district attorney, who cross-examined him as to every detail of his beliefs, and read garbled extracts from his published writings, in the effort to make it appear that he held some belief which might possibly prejudice the jury against him. The defendant in this case, a returned soldier who had spent three years as a volunteer in the trenches, and had been twice wounded and once gassed, was accused, not merely of approving the Soviet form of government, but also of having printed uncomplimentary references to priests and religious institutions.

Nowadays it is the propertied class which has taken possession of the powers of government, and which presumes to censor the thinking of mankind in its own interest. But whether it be priestcraft or whether it be capitalism which seeks to bind the human mind, it comes to the same thing, and the effort must be met by the assertion that, in spite of errors and blunders, and the serious harm these may do, there is no way for men to advance save by using the best powers of thinking they possess, and proclaiming their conclusions to others. Speaking theologically for the moment, God has given us our reasoning powers, and also the impulse to use them, and it is inconceivable that He should seek to restrict their use, or should give to anyone the power to forbid their use. It is His truth which we seek, and His which we proclaim. In so doing we perform our highest act of faith, and we refuse to be troubled by the idea that for this service He will reward us by an eternity of sulphur and brimstone.

Throughout the remainder of this book it will be assumed that the reader accepts this point of view, or, at any rate, that he is willing for purposes of experiment to give it a trial and see where it leads him. We shall proceed to consider the problems of human life in the light of reason, to determine how they come to be, and how they can be solved.

CHAPTER IV

THE ORIGIN OF MORALITY

(Compares the ways of nature with human morality, and tries to show how the latter came to be.)

Seventy years ago Charles Darwin published his book, "The Origin of Species," in which he defied the theological dogma of his time by the shocking idea that life had evolved by many stages of progress from the diatom to man. This of course did not conform to the story of the Garden of Eden, and so "Darwinism" was fought as an invention of the devil, and in the interior of America there are numerous sectarian colleges where the dread term "evolution" is spoken in awed whispers. Only the other day I read in my newspaper the triumphant proclamation of some clergyman that "Darwinism" had been overthrown. This reverend gentleman had got mixed up because some biologists were disputing some detail of the method by which the evolution of species had been brought about. Do species change by the gradual elimination of the unfit, or do they change by sudden leaps, the "mutation" theory of de Vries? Are acquired powers transmitted to posterity, or is the germ plasm unaffected by its environment? Concerning such questions the scientists debate. But the fact that life has evolved in an ordered series from the lower forms to the higher, and that each individual reproduces in embryo and in infancy the history of this long process—these facts are now the basis of all modern thinking, and as generally accepted as the rotation of the earth.

You may study this process of evolution from the outside, in the multitude of forms which it has assumed and in their reactions one to another; or you may study it from the inside in your own soul, the emotions which accompany it, the impulse or craving which impels it, the *élan vital*, as it is called by the French philosopher Bergson. The Christians call it love, and Nietzsche, who hated Christianity, called it "the will to power," and persuaded himself that it was the opposite of love.

You will find in the essays of Professor Huxley, one entitled "Evolution and Ethics," in which he sets forth the complete unmorality of nature, and declares that there is no way by which what mankind knows as morality can have originated in the process of nature or can be reconciled to natural law. This statement, coming from a leading agnostic, was welcome to the theologians. But when I first read the essay, as a student of sixteen, it seemed to me narrow; I thought I saw a standpoint from which the contradiction disappeared. The difference between the morality of Christ and the morality of nature is merely the difference between a lower and a higher stage of mental development. The animal loves and seeks by instinct to preserve the life which it knows—that is to say, its own life and the life of its young. The wolf knows nothing about the feelings of a deer; but man in his savage state develops reasoning powers enough to realize that there are others like himself, the members of his own tribe, and he makes for himself taboos which forbid him to kill and eat the members of that tribe. At the present time humanity has developed its reason and imaginative sympathy to include in the "tribe" one or two hundred million people; while to those outside the tribe it still preserves the attitude of the wolf.

How came it that a mind so acute as Huxley's went so far astray on the question of the evolution of morality? The answer is that this was the factory age in England, and the great scientist, a rebel in theological matters, was in economics a child of his time. We find him using the formulas of bourgeois biology to ridicule Henry George and his plea for the freeing of the land. "Competition is the life of trade," ran the nineteenth century slogan; and competition was the god of nineteenth century biology. Tennyson summed it up in the phrase: "Nature red in tooth and claw with ravin;" and this was found convenient by Manchester manufacturers who wished to shut little children up for fourteen hours a day in cotton mills, and to harness women to drag cars in the coal mines, and to be told by the learned men of their colleges and the holy men of their churches that this was "the survival of the fittest," it was nature's way of securing the advancement of the race.

But now we are preparing for an era of cooperation, and it occurs to our men of science to go back to nature and find out what really are her ways. If you will read Kropotkin's "Mutual Aid as a Factor in Evolution," you will find a complete refutation of the old bourgeois biology, and a view of nature which reveals in it the germs of human morality. Kropotkin points out that everywhere throughout nature it is the social and not the solitary animals which are most numerous and most successful. There are many millions of ants and bees for every hawk or eagle, and certainly in the state of nature there were thousands of deer for every lion or tiger that preyed upon them. And all these social creatures have their ways of being, which it requires no stress of the imagination to compare with the tribal customs and the moral codes of mankind. The different animals prey upon one another, but they do not prey upon their own species, except in a few rare cases. The only beast that makes a regular practice of exploiting his own kind is man.

By hundreds of interesting illustrations Kropotkin shows that mutual aid and mutual self-protection are the means whereby the higher forms of being have been evolved. Insects and birds and fish, nearly all the herbivorous mammals, and even a great many of the carnivores, help one another and protect one another. The chattering monkeys in the treetops drove out the saber-tooth tiger from the grove because there were so many of them, and when they saw him they all set up a shriek and clamor which deafened and confused him. And when by and by these monkeys developed an opposed thumb, and broke off a branch of a tree for a club, and fastened a sharp stone on the end of it for an axe, and fell upon the saber-toothed tiger and exterminated him, they did it because they had learned solidarity—even as the workers of the world are today learning solidarity in the face of the beast of capitalism.

Man has survived by the cunning of his brain, we are told, and that is true. But first among the products of that cunning brain has been the knowledge that by himself he is the most helpless and pitiful of creatures, while standing together and forming societies and developing moralities, he is master of the world. He has not yet learned that lesson entirely; he has learned it only for his own nation. Therefore he takes the highest skill of his hand and the subtlest wit of his brain, and uses them to manufacture poison gases. At the present hour he is painfully realizing that his poison formulas all become known to the tribes whom he calls his enemies, and so it is his own destruction he is engaged in contriving. In other words, man has come to a time when his mechanical skill, his mastery over the forces of nature, has developed more rapidly than his moral sense and his imaginative sympathy. His ability to destroy life has become dangerously greater than his desire to preserve it. So he confronts the fair face of nature as an insane creature, wrecking not merely everything that he himself has built up, but everything that nature has built in the ages before him. He is striving now with infinite agony to make this fact real to himself, and to mend his evil ways; and the first step in that process is to root out from his mind the devil's doctrine which in his blindness and greed he has himself implanted, that there is any way for him to find real happiness, or to make any worth while progress on this earth, by the method of inflicting misery and torment upon his fellow men.

CHAPTER V

NATURE AND MAN

(Attempts to show how man has taken control of nature, and is carrying on her processes and improving upon them.)

If the argument of the preceding chapter is sound, human morality is not a fixed and eternal set of laws, but is, like everything else in the world, a product of natural evolution. We can trace the history of it, just as we trace the story of the rocks. It is not a mysterious or supernatural thing, it is simply the reaction of man to his environment, and more especially to his fellow men. The source of it is that same inner impulse, that love of life, that joy in growing, that faith which appears to be the soul of all being.

Man is a part of nature and a product of nature; in many fundamental respects his ways are still nature's ways and his laws still nature's laws. But there are other and even more significant ways in which man has separated himself from nature and made himself something quite different. In order to reveal this clearly, we draw a distinction between nature and man. This is a proper thing to do, provided we bear in mind that our classification is not permanent or final. We distinguish frogs from tadpoles, in spite of the fact that at one stage the creature is half tadpole and half frog. We distinguish the animal from the vegetable kingdom, despite the fact that in their lower forms they cannot be distinguished.

What, precisely, is the difference between nature and man? The difference lies in the fact that nature is apparently blind in her processes; she produces a million eggs in order to give life to one salmon, she produces countless millions of salmon to be devoured by other fish apparently no better than salmon. Poets may take up the doctrine of evolution and dress it out in theological garments, talking about the "one far off divine event towards which the whole creation moves," but for all we can see, nature, apart from man, is just as well satisfied to move in circles, and to come back exactly where she started. Nature made a whole world of complicated creatures in the steamy, luke-warm swamps of the Mesozoic era, and then, as if deciding that the pattern of a large body and a small brain was not a success, she froze them all to death with a glacial epoch, and we have nothing but the bones to tell us about them.

No one understands anything about evolution until he has realized that the phrase "the survival of the fittest" does not mean the survival of the best from any human point of view. It merely means the survival of those capable of surviving in some particular environment. We consider our present civilization as "fit"; but if astronomical changes should cause another ice age, we should discover that our "fitness" depended upon our ability to live on lichens, or on something we could grow by artificial light in the bowels of the earth.

So much for our ancient mother, nature. But now—whether we say with the theologians that it was divine providence, or with the materialist philosophers that it was an accidental mixing of atoms—at any rate it has come about that nature has recently produced creatures who are conscious of her process, who are able to observe and criticize it, to take up her work and carry it on in their own way, for better or for worse. Whether by accident or design, there has been on parts of our planet such a combination of climate and soil as has brought into being a new product of nature, a heightened form of life which we call "intelligence." Creation opens its eyes, and beholds the work of the creator, and decides that it is good—yet not so good as it might be! Creation takes up the work of the creator, and continues it, in many respects annulling it, in other respects revising it entirely. Whether a sonnet is a better or a higher product than a spider is a question it would be futile to discuss; but this, at least, should be clear— nature has produced an infinity of spiders, but nature never produced a sonnet, nor anything resembling it.

Man, the creature of God, takes over the functions of God. This fact may shock us, or it may inspire us; to the metaphysically minded it offers a great variety of fascinating problems. Can it be that God is in process of becoming, that there is no God until he has become, in us and through us? H. G. Wells sets forth this curious idea; and then, of course, the bishops and the clergy rise up in indignation and denounce Mr. Wells as an upstart and trespasser upon their field. They have been worshipping their God for some three or four thousand years, and know that He has been from eternity; He created the world at His will, and how shall impious man presume to rise up and criticize His product, and imagine that he can improve upon it? Man, with his cheap and silly little toys, his sonnets and scientific systems, his symphony concerts and such pale imitations of celestial harmonies!

Mr. Wells, in his character of God in the making, has created a bishop of his own, and no doubt would maintain the thesis that he is a far better bishop than any created by the God of the Anglican churches. We will leave Mr. Wells' bishop to argue these problems with God's bishops, and will merely remind the reader of our warning about these metaphysical matters. You can prove anything and everything, whichever and however, all or both; and discussions of the subject are merely your enunciation of the fact that you have your private truth as you want it. It may be that there is an Infinite Consciousness, which carries the whole process of creation in itself, and that all the seeming wastes and blunders of nature can be explained from some point of view at present beyond the reach of our minds. On the other hand it may be that consciousness is now dawning in the universe for the first time. It may be that it is an accident, a fleeting product like the morning mist on the mountain top. On the other hand, it may be that it is destined to grow and expand and take control of the entire universe, as a farmer takes control of a field for his own purposes. It may be that just as our individual fragments of intelligence communicate and merge into a family, a club, a nation, a world culture, so we shall some day grope our way toward the consciousness of other planets, or of other states of being subsisting on this planet unknown to us, or perhaps even toward the cosmic soul, the universal consciousness which we call God.

But meantime, all we can say with positiveness is this: man, the created, is becoming the creator. He is taking up the world purpose, he is imposing upon it new purposes of his own, he is attempting to impose upon it a moral code, to test it and discipline it by a new standard which he calls economy. To the present writer this seems the most significant fact about life, the most fascinating point of view from which life can be regarded. The reader who wishes to follow it into greater detail is referred to a little book by Professor E. Ray Lankester, "The Kingdom of Man"; especially the opening essay, with its fascinating title, "Nature's Insurgent Son."

In what ways have the reasoned and deliberate purposes of man revised and even supplanted the processes of nature? The ways are so many that it would be easier to mention those in which he has not done so. A modern civilized man is hardly content with anything that nature does, nor willing to accept any of nature's products. He will not eat nature's fruits, he prefers the kinds that he himself has brought into being. He is not content with the skin that nature has given him; he has made himself an infinite variety of complicated coverings. He objects to nature's habit of pouring cold water upon him, and so he has built himself houses in which he makes his own climate; he has recently taken to creating for himself houses which roll along the ground, or which fly through the air, or which swim under the surface of the sea; so he carries his private climate with him to all these places. It was nature's custom to remove her blunders and her experiments quickly from her sight. But man has decided that he loves life so well that he will preserve even the imbeciles, the lame and the halt and the blind. In a state of nature, if a man's eyes were not properly focused, he blundered into the lair of a tiger and was eaten. But civilized man despises such a method of maintaining the standard of human eyes; he creates for himself a transparent product, ground to such a curve that it corrects the focus of his eyes, and makes them as good as any other eyes. In ten thousand such ways we might name, man has rebelled against the harshness of his ancient mother, and has freed himself from her control.

But still he is the child of his mother, and so it is his way to act first, and then to realize what he has done. So it comes about that very few, even of the most highly educated men, are aware how completely the ancient ways of nature have been suppressed by her "insurgent son." It is a good deal as in the various trades and professions which have developed with such amazing rapidity in modern civilization; the paper man knows how to make paper, the shoe man knows how to make shoes, the optician knows about grinding glasses, but none of these knows very much about the others' specialties, and has no realization of how far the other has gone. So it comes about that in our colleges we are still teaching ancient and immutable "laws of nature," which in the actual practice of men at work are as extinct and forgotten as the dodo. In all colleges, except a few which have been tainted by Socialist thought, the students are solemnly learning the so-called "Malthusian law," that population presses continually upon the limits of subsistence, there are always a few more people in every part of the world than that part of the world is able to maintain. At any time we increase the world's productive powers, population will increase correspondingly, so there can never be an end to human misery, and abortion, war and famine are simply nature's eternal methods of adjusting man to his environment.

Thus solemnly we are taught in the colleges. And yet, nine out of ten of the students come from homes where the parents have discovered the modern practice of birth control; all the students are themselves finding out about it in one way or another, and will proceed when they marry to restrict themselves to two or three children. In vain will the ghost of their favorite statesman and hero, Theodore Roosevelt, be traveling up and down the land, denouncing them for the dreadful crime of "race suicide"—that is to say, their presuming to use their reason to put an end to the ghastly situation revealed by the Malthusian law, over-population eternally recurring and checked by abortion, war and famine! In vain will the ghost of their favorite saint and moralist, Anthony Comstock, be traveling up and down the land, putting people in jail for daring to teach to poor women what every rich woman knows, and for attempting to change the entirely man-made state of affairs whereby an intelligent and self-governing Anglo-Saxon land is being in two or three generations turned over to a slum population of Italians, Poles, Hungarians, Portuguese, French-Canadians, Mexicans and Japanese!

Likewise in every orthodox college the student is taught what his professors are pleased to call "the law of diminishing returns of agriculture." That is to say, additional labor expended upon a plot of land does not result in an equal increase of produce, and the increase grows less, until finally you come to a time when no matter how much labor you expend, you can get no more produce from that plot of land. All professors teach this, because fifty years ago it was true, and since that time it has not occurred to any professor of political science to visit a farm. And all the while, out in the suburbs of the city where the college is located, market gardeners are practicing on an enormous scale a new system of intensive agriculture which makes the "law of diminishing returns" a foolish joke.

As Kropotkin shows in his book, "Fields, Factories and Workshops," the modern intensive gardener, by use of glass and the chemical test-tube, has developed an entirely new science of plant raising. He is independent of climate, he makes his own climate; he is independent of the defects of the soil, he would just as soon start from nothing and make his soil upon an asphalt pavement. By doubling his capital investment he raises, not twice as much produce, but ten times as much. If his methods were applied to the British Isles, he could raise sufficient produce on this small surface to feed the population of the entire globe.

So we see that by simple and entirely harmless devices man is in position to restrict or to increase population as he sees fit. Also he is in position to raise food and produce the necessities of life for a hundred or thousand times as many people as are now on the earth. But superstition ordains involuntary parenthood, and capitalism ordains that land shall be held out of use for speculation, or shall be exploited for rent! And this is done in the name of "nature"—that old nature of the "tooth and claw," whose ancient plan it is "that they shall take who have the power, and they shall keep who can"; that ancient nature which has been so entirely suppressed and supplanted by civilized man, and which survives only as a ghost, a skeleton to be resurrected from the tomb, for the purpose of frightening the enslaved. When a predatory financier wishes a fur overcoat to protect himself from the cold, or when he hires a masseur to keep up the circulation of his blood, you do not find him troubling himself about the laws of "nature"; never will he mention this old scarecrow, except when he is trying to persuade the workers of the world to go on paying him tribute for the use of the natural resources of the earth!

CHAPTER VI

MAN THE REBEL

(Shows the transition stage between instinct and reason, in which man finds himself, and how he can advance to a securer condition.)

In the state of nature you find every creature living a precarious existence, incessantly beset by enemies; and the creature survives only so long as it keeps itself at the top of its form. The result is the maintenance of the type in its full perfection, and, under the competitive pressure, a gradual increase of its powers. Excepting when sudden eruptions of natural forces occur, every creature is perfectly provided with a set of instincts for all emergencies; it is in harmonious relationship to its environment, it knows how to do what it has to do, and even its fears and its pains serve for its protection. But now comes man and overthrows this state of nature, abolishes the competitive struggle, and changes at his own insolent will both his environment and his reaction thereto.

Man's changes are, in the beginning, all along one line; they are for his own greater comfort, the avoidance of the inconveniences of nature and the stresses of the competitive struggle. In a state of nature there are no fat animals, but in civilization there are not merely fat animals, but fat men to eat the fat animals. In a state of nature no animal loafs very long; it has to go out and hunt its food again. But man, by his superior cunning, compels the animals to work for him, and also his fellow men. So he produces unlimited wealth for himself; not merely can he eat and drink and sleep all he wants, but he builds a whole elaborate set of laws and moral customs and religious codes about this power, he invents manners and customs and literatures and arts, expressive of his superiority to nature and to his fellow men, and of his ability to enslave and exploit them. So he destroys for his imperious self the beneficent guardianship which nature had maintained over him; he develops a thousand complicated diseases, a thousand monstrous abnormalities of body and mind and spirit. And each one of these diseases and abnormalities is a new life of its own; it develops a body of knowledge, a science, and perhaps an art; it becomes the means of life, the environment and the determining destiny of thousands, perhaps millions, of human beings. So continues the growth of the colossal structure which we call civilization—in part still healthy and progressive, but in part as foul and deadly as a gigantic cancer.

What is to be done about this cancer? First of all, it must be diagnosed, the extent of it precisely mapped out and the causes of it determined. Man, the rebel, has rejected his mother nature, and has lost and for the most part forgotten the instincts with which she provided him. He has destroyed the environment which, however harsh to the individual, was beneficent to the race, and has set up in the place of it a gigantic pleasure-house, with talking machines and moving pictures and soda fountains and manicure parlors and "gents' furnishing establishments."

Shall we say that man is to go back to a state of nature, that he shall no longer make asylums for the insane and homes for the defective, eye-glasses for the astigmatic and malted milk for the dyspeptic? There are some who preach that. Among the multitude of strange books and pamphlets which come in my mail, I found the other day a volume from England, "Social Chaos and the Way Out," by Alfred Baker Read, a learned and imposing tome of 364 pages, wherein with all the paraphernalia of learning it is gravely maintained that the solution for the ills of civilization is a return to the ancient Greek practice of infanticide. Every child at birth is to be examined by a committee of physicians, and if it is found to possess any defect, or if the census has established that there are enough babies in the world for the present, this baby shall be mercifully and painlessly asphyxiated. You might think that this is a joke, after the fashion of Swift's proposal for eating the children of famine-stricken Ireland. I have spent some time examining this book before I risk committing myself to the statement that it is the work of a sober scientist, with no idea whatever of fun.

If we are going to think clearly on this subject, the first point we have to understand is that nature has nothing to do with it. We cannot appeal to nature, because we are many thousands of years beyond her sway. We left her when the first ape came down from the treetop and fastened a sharp stone in the end of his club; we bade irrevocable good-bye to her when the first man kept himself from freezing and altered his diet by means of fire. Therefore, it is no argument to say that this, that, or the other remedy is "unnatural." Our choice will lie among a thousand different courses, but the one thing we may be sure of is that none of them will be "natural." Bairnsfather, in one of his war cartoons, portrays a British officer on leave, who got homesick for the trenches and went out into the garden and dug himself a hole in the mud and sat shivering in the rain all night. And this amuses us vastly; but we should be even more amused if any kind of reformer, physician, moralist, clergyman or legislator should suggest to us any remedy for our ills that was really "according to nature."

Civilized man, creature of art and of knowledge, has no love for nature except as an object for the play of his fancy and his wit. He means to live his own life, he means to hold himself above nature with all his powers. Yet, obviously, he cannot go on accumulating diseases, he cannot give his life-blood to the making of a cancer while his own proper tissues starve. He must somehow divert the flow of his energies, his social blood-stream, so to speak, from the cancer to the healthy growth. To abandon the metaphor, man will determine by the use of his reason what he wishes life to be; he will choose the highest forms of it to which he can attain. He will then, by the deliberate act of his own will, devote his energies to those tasks; he will make for himself new laws, new moral codes, new customs and ways of thought, calculated to bring to reality the ideal which he has formed. So only can man justify himself as a creator, so can he realize the benefit and escape the penalties of his revolt from his ancient mother.

And then, perhaps, we shall make the discovery that we have come back to nature, only in a new form. Nature, harsh and cruel, wasteful and blind as we call her, yet had her deep wisdom; she cared for the species, she protected and preserved the type. Man, in his new pride of power, has invented a philosophy which he dignifies by the name of "individualism." He lives and works for himself; he chooses to wear silk shirts, and to break the speed limit, and to pin ribbons and crosses on his chest. Now what he must do with his new morality, if he wishes to save himself from degeneration, is to manifest the wisdom and far vision of the old mother whom he spurned, and to say to himself, deliberately, as an act of high daring: I will protect the species, I will preserve the type! I will deny myself the raptures of alcoholic intoxication, because it damages the health of my offspring; I will deny myself the amusement of sexual promiscuity for the same reason. I will devise imitations of the chase and of battle in order that I may keep my physical body up to the best standard of nature. Because I understand that all civilized life is based upon intelligence, I will acquire knowledge and spread it among my fellow men. Because I perceive that civilization is impossible without sympathy, and because sympathy makes it impossible for me to be happy while my fellow men are ignorant and degraded, therefore I dedicate my energies to the extermination of poverty, war, parasitism and all forms of exploitation of man by his fellows.

Professor William James is the author of an excellent essay entitled "A Moral Equivalent for War." He sets forth the idea that men have loved war through the ages because it has called forth their highest efforts, has made them more fully aware of the powers of their being. He asks, May it not be possible for man, of his own free impulse, born of his love of life and the wonderful potentialities which it unfolds, to invent for himself a discipline, a code based, not upon the destruction of other men and their enslavement, but upon cooperative emulation in the unfoldment of the powers of the mind? That this can be done by men, I have never doubted. That it will be done, and done quickly, has been made certain by the late world conflict, which has demonstrated to all thinking people that the progress of the mechanical arts has been such that man is now able to inflict upon his own civilization more damage than it is able to endure.

CHAPTER VII

MAKING OUR MORALS

(Attempts to show that human morality must change to fit human facts, and there can be no judge of it save human reason.)

Assuming the argument of the preceding chapters to be accepted, it appears that human life is in part at least a product of human will, guided by human intelligence. Man finds himself in the position of the crew of a ship in the middle of the ocean; he does not know exactly how the ship was made, or how it came to be in its present position, but he has discovered how the engines are run, and how the ship is steered, and the meaning of the compass. So now he takes charge of the ship, and keeps it afloat amid many perils; and meantime, on the bridge of the vessel, there goes on a furious argument over the question what port the ship shall be steered to and what chart shall be used.

It is not well as a rule to trust to similes, but this simile is useful because it helps us to realize how fluid and changeable are the conditions of man's life, and how incessant and urgent the problems with which he finds himself confronted. The moral and legal codes of mankind may be compared to the steering orders which are given to the helmsman of the vessel. Northeast by north, he is told; and if during the night a heavy wind arises, and pushes the bow of the vessel off to starboard, then the helmsman has to push the wheel in the opposite direction. If he does not do so, he may find that his vessel has swung around and is going to some other part of the world. Next morning the passengers may wake up and find the ship on the rocks— because the helmsman persisted in following certain steering directions which were laid down in an ancient Hebrew book two or three thousand years ago!

If life is a continually changing product, then the laws which govern conduct must also be continually changing, and morality is a problem of continuous adjustment to new circumstances and new needs. If man is free to work upon this changing environment, he must be free to make new tools and devise new processes. If it is the task of reason to choose among many possible courses and many possible varieties of life, then clearly it is man's duty to examine and revise every detail of his laws and customs and moral codes.

This is, of course, in flat contradiction to the teachings of all religions. So far as I know there is no religion which does not teach that the conduct of man in certain matters has been eternally fixed by some higher power, and that it is man's duty to conform to these rules. It is considered to be wicked even to suggest any other idea; in fact, to do so is the most wicked thing in the world, far more dangerous than any actual infraction of the code, whatever it may be.

Let us see how this works out in practice. Let us take, for a test, the Ten Commandments. These commandments were graven upon stone tablets some four thousand years ago, and are supposed to have been valid ever since. "Thou shalt not kill," is one; others phrase it, "Thou shall do no murder"; and in this double version we see at once the beginnings of controversy. If you are a Quaker, you accept the former version, while if you are a member of the military general staff of your country you accept the latter. You maintain the right to kill your fellow men, provided that those who do the killing have been previously clad in a special uniform, indicating their distinctive function as killers of their fellow men. You maintain, in other words, the right of making war; and presently, when you get into making war, you find yourself maintaining the right to kill, not merely by the old established method of the sword and the bullet, but by means of poison gases which destroy the lives of women and children, perhaps a whole city full at a time.

And also, of course, you maintain the right to kill, provided the killing has been formally ordered and sanctioned by a man who sits upon a raised bench and wears a black robe, and perhaps a powdered wig. You consider that by the simple device of putting this man into a black robe and a powdered wig, you endow him with authority to judge and revise the divine law. In other words, you subject this divine law to human reason; and if some religious fanatic refuses to be so subjected, you call him by the dread name "pacifist," and if he attempts to preach his idea, you send him to prison for ten or twenty years, which means in actual practice that you kill him by the slow effects of malnutrition and tubercular infection. If he is ordered to put on the special costume of killing, and refuses to do so, you call him a "C. O.," and you bully and beat him, and perhaps administer to him the "water cure" in your dungeons.

Or take the commandment that we shall not commit adultery. Surely this is a law about which we can agree! But presently we discover that unhappily married couples desire to part, and that if we do not allow them to part, we actually cause the commission of a great deal more adultery than otherwise. Therefore, our wise men meet together, and revise this divine law, and decide that it is not adultery if a man takes another wife, provided he has received from a judge an engraved piece of paper permitting him to do so. But some of the followers of religion refuse to admit this right of mere mortal man. The Catholic Church attempts to enforce its own laws, and declares that people who divorce and remarry are really living in adultery and committing mortal sin. The Episcopal Church does not go quite so far as that; it allows the innocent party in the divorce to remarry. Other churches are content to accept the state law as it stands. Is it not manifest that all these groups are applying human reason, and nothing but human reason, to the interpreting and revising of their divine commandments?

Or take the law, "Thou shalt not steal." Surely we can all agree upon that! Let us do so; but our agreement gets us nowhere, because we have to set up a human court to decide what is "stealing." Is it stealing to seize upon land, and kill the occupants of it, and take the land for your own, and hand it down to your children forever? Yes, of course, that is stealing, you say; but at once you have to revise your statement. It is not stealing if it was done a sufficient number of years ago; in that case the results of it are sanctified by law, and held unchangeable forever. Also, we run up against the fact that it is not stealing, if it is done by the State, by men who have been dressed up in the costume of killers before they commit the act.

Again, is it stealing to hold land out of use for speculation, while other men are starving and dying for lack of land to labor upon? Some of us call this stealing, but we are impolitely referred to as "radicals," and if we venture to suggest that anyone should resist this kind of stealing, we are sentenced to slow death from malnutrition and tubercular infection. Again, is it stealing for a victim of our system of land monopoly to take a loaf of bread in order to save the life of his starving child? The law says that this is stealing, and sends the man to jail for this act; yet the common sense of mankind protests, and I have heard a great many respectable Americans venture so far in "radicalism" as to say that they themselves would steal under such circumstances.

One could pile up illustrations without limit; but this is enough to make clear the point, that it is perfectly futile to attempt to talk about "divine" rules for human conduct. Regardless of any ideas you may hold, or any wishes, you are forced at every hour of your life to apply your reason to the problems of your life, and you have no escape from the task of judging and deciding. All that you do is to judge right or to judge wrong; and if you judge wrong, you inflict misery upon yourself and upon all who come into contact with you. How much more sensible, therefore, to recognize the fact of moral and intellectual responsibility; to investigate the data of life with which you have to deal, the environment by which you are surrounded, and to train your judgment so that you will be able to fit yourself to it with quickness and certainty!

"But," the believer in religion will say, "this leaves mankind without any guide or authority. How can human beings act, how can they deal with one another, if there are no laws, no permanent moral codes?"

The answer is that to accept the idea of the evolution of morality does not mean at all that there will be no permanent laws and working principles. Many of the facts of life are fixed for all practical purposes—the purposes not merely of your life and my life, but the life of many generations. We are not likely to see in our time the end of the ancient Hebrew announcement that "the sins of the father are visited upon the children"; therefore it is possible for us to study out a course of action based upon the duty of every father to hand down to his children the gift of a sound mind in a sound body. The Catholic Church has had for a thousand years or more the "mortal sin" of gluttony upon its list; and today comes experimental science with its new weapons of research, and discovers autointoxication and the hardening of the arteries, and makes it very unlikely that the moral codes of men will ever fail to list gluttony as a mortal sin. Indeed, science has added to gluttony, not merely drunkenness, but all use of alcoholic liquor for beverage purposes; we have done this in spite of the manifest fact that the drinking of wine was not merely an Old Testament virtue, but a New Testament religious rite.

To say that human life changes, and that new discoveries and new powers make necessary new laws and moral customs, is to say something so obvious that it might seem a waste of paper and ink. Man has invented the automobile and has crowded himself into cities, and so has to adopt a rigid set of traffic regulations. So far as I know, it has never occurred to any religious enthusiast to seek in the book of Revelation for information as to the advisability of the "left hand turn" at Broadway and Forty-second Street, New York, at five o'clock in the afternoon. But modern science has created new economic facts, just as unprecedented as the automobile; it has created new possibilities of spending and new possibilities of starving for mankind; it has made new cravings and new satisfactions, new crimes and new virtues; and yet the great mass of our people are still seeking to guide themselves in their readjustments to these new facts by ancient codes which have no more relationship to these facts than they have to the affairs of Mars!

I am acquainted with a certain lady, one of the kindest and most devoted souls alive, who seeks to solve the problems of her life, and of her large family of children and grand-children, according to sentences which she picks out, more or less at random, from certain more or less random chapters of ancient Hebrew literature. This lady will find some words which she imagines apply to the matter, and will shut her devout eyes to the fact that there are other "texts," bearing on the matter, which say exactly the opposite. She will place the strangest and most unimaginable interpretations upon the words, and yet will be absolutely certain that her interpretation is the voice of God speaking directly to her. If you try to tell her about Socialism, she will say, "The poor ye have always with you"; which means that it is interfering with Divine Providence to try to remedy poverty on any large scale. This lady is ready instantly to relieve any single case of want; she regards it as her duty to do this; in fact, she considers that the purpose of some people's poverty is to provide her with a chance to do the noble action of relieving it. You would think that the meaning of the sentence, "Spare the rod and spoil the child," would be so plain that no one could mistake it; but this good lady understood it to mean that God forbade the physical chastisement of children, and preferred them "spoiled." She held this idea for half a lifetime—until it was pointed out to her that the sentence was not in the Bible, but in "Hudibras," an old English poem!

CHAPTER VIII

THE VIRTUE OF MODERATION

(Attempts to show that wise conduct is an adjustment of means to ends, and depends upon the understanding of a particular set of circumstances.)

Some years ago I used to know an ardent single tax propagandist who found my way of arguing intensely irritating, because, as he phrased it, I had "no principles." We would be discussing, for example, a protective tariff, and I would wish to collect statistics, but discovered to my bewilderment that to my single tax friend a customs duty was "stealing" on the part of the government. The government had a right to tax land, because that was the gift of nature, but it had no right to tax the products of human labor, and when it took a portion of the goods which anyone brought into a country, the government was playing the part of a robber. Of course such a man was annoyed by the suggestion that in the early stages of a country's development it might possibly be a good thing for the country to make itself independent and self-sufficient by encouraging the development of its manufactures; that, on the other hand, when these manufactures had grown to such a size that they controlled the government, it might be an excellent thing for the country to subject them to the pressure of foreign competition, in order to lower their value as a preliminary to socializing them.

The reader who comes to this book looking for hard and fast rules of life will be disappointed. It would be convenient if someone could lay down for us a moral code, and lift from our shoulders the inconvenient responsibility of deciding about our own lives. There may be persons so weak that they have to have the conditions of their lives thus determined for them; but I am not writing for such persons. I am writing for adult and responsible individuals, and I bear in mind that every individual is a separate problem, with separate needs and separate duties. There are, of course, a good many rules that apply to everybody in almost all emergencies, but I cannot think of a single rule that I would be willing to say I would apply in my life without a single exception. "Thou shalt not kill" is a rule that I have followed, so far without exception; but as soon as I turn my imagination loose, I can think of many circumstances under which I should kill. I remember discussing the matter with a pacifist friend of mine, an out-and-out religious non-resistant. I pointed out to him that people sometimes went insane, and in that condition they sometimes seized hatchets and killed anyone in sight. What would my pacifist friend do if he saw a maniac attacking his children with a hatchet? It did not help him to say that he would use all possible means short of killing the maniac; he had finally to admit that if he were quite sure it was a question of the life of the maniac or the life of his child, he would kill. And this is not mere verbal quibbling, because such things do happen in the world, and people are confronted with such emergencies, and they have to decide, and no rule is a general rule if it has a single exception. There is a saying that "the exception proves the rule," but this is very silly; it is a mistranslation of the Latin word "probat," which means, not proves, but tests. No exception can prove a rule. What the exception does is to test the rule by showing that the result does not follow in the exceptional case.

The only kind of rule which can be laid down for human conduct is a rule in such general terms that it escapes exceptions by leaving the matter open for every man's difference of opinion. Any kind of rule which is specific will sooner or later pass out of date. Take, by way of illustration, the ancient and well-established virtue of frugality. Obviously, under a state of nature, or of economic competition, it is necessary for every man to lay by a store "for a rainy day." But suppose we could set up a condition of economic security, under which society guaranteed to every man the full product of his labor, and the old and the sick were fully taken care of—then how foolish a man would seem who troubled to acquire a surplus of goods! It would be as if we saw him riding on horseback through the main street of our town in a full suit of armor!

I devote a good deal of space to this question of a fixed and unchangeable morality, because it is one of the heaviest burdens that mankind carries upon its back. The record of human history is sickening, not so much because of blood and slaughter, but because of fanaticism; because wherever the mind of man attempts to assert itself, to escape from the blind rule of animal greed, it adopts a set of formulas, and proceeds to enforce them, regardless of consequences, upon the whole of life. Consider, for example, the rule of the Puritans in England. The Puritans glorified conscience, and it is perfectly proper to glorify conscience, but not to the entire suppression of the beauty-making faculties in man. Macaulay summed up the Puritan point of view in the sentence that they objected to bear-baiting, not because it gave pain to the bear, but because it gave pleasure to the spectators. As a result of applying that principle, and lacing mankind in a straight-jacket by legislation, England swung back into a reaction under the Cavaliers, in which debauchery held more complete sway than ever before or since in English life.

This is a hard lesson, but it must be learned: there is no virtue that does not become a vice if it is carried to extremes; there is no virtue that does not become a vice if it is applied at the wrong time, or under the wrong circumstances, or at the wrong stage of human development. In fact, we may say that most vices are virtues misapplied. The so-called natural vices are simply natural impulses carried to excess, while the unnatural vices result from the suppression and distortion of natural impulses. The Greeks had as their supreme virtue what they called "sophrosuné." It is a beautiful word, worth remembering; it means a beautiful quality called moderation. We shall find, as we come to investigate, that life is a series of compromises among many different needs, many different desires, many different duties; and reason sits as a wise and patient judge, and appoints to each its proper portion, and denies to it an excess which would starve the others. Such is true morality, and it is incompatible with the existence of any fixed code, whether of human origin or divine.

The fixed morality is a survival of a far-off past, of the days of instinct and servitude. Human reason has developed but slowly, and perhaps only a few people are as yet entirely capable of taking control of their own destiny; perhaps it is really dangerous to think for oneself! But if we investigate carefully, we may decide that the danger is not so much to ourselves as it is to others. The most evil of all the habits that man has inherited from his far-off past is the habit of exploiting his fellows, and in order to exploit them more safely the ruling castes of priests and kings and nobles and property owners have taken possession of the moralities of the world and shaped them for their own convenience. They have taught the slave virtues of credulity and submission; they have surrounded their teachings with all the terrors of the supernatural; they have placed upon rebellion the penalties, not merely of this world, but of the next, not merely of the dungeon and the rack, but of hellfire and brimstone.

I do not wish to go to extremes and say that the moral codes now taught in the world are made wholly in this evil way. As a matter of fact they are a queer jumble of the two elements, the slave terrors of the past and the common sense of the present. There is not one moral code in the world today, there are many. There is one for the rich, and an entirely different one for the poor, and the rich have had a great deal more to do with shaping the code of the poor than the poor have had to do with shaping the code of the rich. There is one code for governments, and an entirely different one for the victims of governments. There is one code for business, and an entirely different one, a far more human and decent one, for friendship. Above all, there is one code for Sunday and another code for the other six days of the week. Most of our idealisms and our sentimental fine phrases we reserve for our Sunday code, while for our every-day code we go back to the rule of the jungle: "Dog eat dog," or "Do unto others as they would do unto you, but do it first." When you attempt to suggest a new moral code to our present day moral authorities, it is the fine phrases of the Sunday code they bring out for exhibition purposes; and perhaps you are impressed by their arguments—until Monday morning, when you attempt to apply this code at the office, and they stare at you in bewilderment, or burst out laughing in your face.

What I am trying to do here is to outline a code that will not be a matter of phrases but a matter of practice. It will apply to all men, rich as well as poor, and to all seven days of the week. I am not so much suggesting a code, as pointing out to you how you can work out your own code for yourself. I am suggesting that you should adopt it, not because I tell you to, but because you yourself have taken it and tested it, precisely as you would test any other of the practical affairs of your life—potatoes as an article of diet, or some particular sack of potatoes that a peddler was trying to sell to you. It is not yet possible for you to be as sure about everything in your life as you can be about a sack of potatoes; human knowledge has not got that far; but at least you can know what is to be known, and if anything is a matter of uncertainty, you can know that. Such knowledge is often the most important of all—just as the driver of an automobile wants to know if a bridge is not to be depended on.

So I say to you that if you want to find happiness in this life, look with distrust upon all absolutes and ultimates, all hard and fast rules, all formulas and dogmas and "general principles." Bear in mind that there are many factors in every case, there are many complications in every human being, there are many sides to every question. Try to keep an open mind and an even temper. Try to take an interest in learning something new every day, and in trying some new experiment. This is the scientific attitude toward life; this is the way of growth and of true success. It is inconvenient, because it involves working your brains, and most people have not been taught to do this, and find it the hardest kind of work there is. But how much better it is to think for yourself, and to protect yourself, than to trust your thinking to some group of people whose only interest may be to exploit you for their advantage!

CHAPTER IX

THE CHOOSING OF LIFE

(Discusses the standards by which we may judge what is best in life, and decide what we wish to make of it.)

We have made the point about evolution, that it may go forward or it may go backward. There is no guarantee in nature that because a thing changes, it must necessarily become better than it was. On the contrary, degeneration is as definitely established a fact as growth, and it is of the utmost importance, in studying the problem of human happiness and how to make it, to get clear the fact that nature has produced, and continues to produce, all kinds of monstrosities and parasites and failures and abortions. And all these blunders of our great mother struggle just as hard, desire life just as ardently as normal creatures, and suffer just as cruelly when they fail. Blind optimism about life is just as fatuous and just as dangerous as blind pessimism, and if we propose to take charge of life, and to make it over, we shall find that we have to get quickly to the task of deciding what our purpose is.

"Choose well, your choice is brief and yet endless," says Carlyle. You are driven in your choice by two facts—first, that you have to choose, regardless of whether you want to or not; and second, that upon your choice depend infinite possibilities of happiness or of misery. The interdependence of life is such that you are choosing not merely for the present, but for the future; you are choosing for your posterity forever, and to some extent you are choosing for all mankind. Matthew Arnold has said that "Conduct is three-fourths of life"; but I, for my part, have never been able to see where he got his figures. It seems to me that conduct is practically everything in life that really counts. Conduct is not merely marriage and birth and premature death; it is not merely eating and drinking and sleeping: it is thinking and aspiring; it is religion and science, music and literature and art. It is not yet the lightning and the cyclone, but with the spread of knowledge it is coming to be these things, and I suspect that some day it may be even the comet and the rising of the sun.

We are now going to apply our reason to this enormous problem of human conduct; we are going to ask ourselves the question: What kind of life do we want? What kind of life are we going to make? What are the standards by which we may know excellence in life, and distinguish it from failure and waste and blunder in life? Obviously, when we have done this, we shall have solved the moral problem; all we shall have to say is, act so that your actions help to bring the desirable things into being, and do not act so as to hinder or weaken them.

We shall not be able to go to nature to settle this question for us. This is our problem, not nature's. But we shall find, as usual, that we can pick up precious hints from her; we shall be wise to study her ways, and learn from her successes and her failures. We are proud of her latest product, ourselves. Let us see how she made us; what were the stages on the way to man?

First in the scale of evolution, it appears, came inert matter. We call it inert, because it looks that way, though we know, of course, that it consists of infinite numbers of molecules vibrating with speed which we can measure even though we cannot imagine it. This "matter" is enormously fascinating, and a wise man will hesitate to speak patronizingly about it. Nevertheless, considering matter apart from the mind which studies it, we decide that it represents a low stage of being. We speak contemptuously of stones and clods and lumps of clay. We award more respect to things like mountains and tempest-tossed oceans, because they are big; in the early days of our race we used to worship these things, but now we think of them merely as the raw material of life, and we should not be in the least interested in becoming a mountain or an ocean.

Almost everyone would agree, therefore, that what we call "life" is a higher and more important achievement of nature. And if we wish to grade this life, we do so according to its sentience—that is to say, the amount and intensity of the consciousness which grows in it. We are interested in the one-celled organisms which swarm everywhere throughout nature, and we study the mysterious processes by which they nourish and beget themselves; we suspect that they have a germ of consciousness in them; but we are surer of the meaning and importance of the consciousness we detect in some complex organism like a fish or bird. We learn to know the signs of consciousness, of dawning intelligence, and we esteem the various kinds of creatures according to the amount of it they possess. We reject mere physical bigness and mere strength. Joyce Kilmer may write:

"Poems are made by men like me,

But only God can make a tree"—

And that seems to us a charming bit of fancy; but the common sense of the thing is voiced to us much better in the lines of old Ben Jonson:

"It is not growing like a tree

In bulk doth make man better be."

If we take two animals of equal bulk, the hippopotamus and the elephant, we shall be far more interested in the elephant, because of the intelligence and what we call "character" which he displays. There are good elephants and bad elephants, kind ones and treacherous ones. We love the dog because we can make a companion of him; that is, because we can teach him to react to human stimuli. Of all animals we are fascinated most by the monkey, because he is nearest to man, and displays the keenest intelligence.

Someone may say that this is all mere human egotism, and that we have no way of really being sure that the life of elephants and hippopotami is not more interesting and significant than the life of men. Never having been either of these animals, I cannot say with assurance; but I know that I have the power to exterminate these creatures, or to pen them in cages, and they are helpless to protect themselves, or even to understand what is happening to them. So I am irresistibly driven to conclude that intelligence is more safe and more worth while than unintelligence; in short, that intelligence is nature's highest product up to date, and that to foster and develop it is the best guess I can make as to the path of wisdom—that is, of intelligence!

When we come to deal with human values, we find that we can trace much the same kind of evolution. Back in the days of the cave man, it was physical strength which dominated the horde; but nowadays, except in the imagination of the small boy, the "strong man" does not cut much of a figure. We go once, perhaps, to see him lift his heavy weights and break his iron bars, but then we are tired of him. Mere strength had to yield in the struggle for life to quickness of eye and hand, to energy which for lack of a better name we may call "nervous." The pugilist who has nothing but muscle goes down before his lighter antagonist who can keep out of his reach, and the crowd loves the football hero who can duck and dodge and make the long runs. One might cite a thousand illustrations, such as the British bowmen breaking down the heavily armored knights, or the quick-moving, light vessels of Britain overcoming the huge galleons of Spain. And as society develops and becomes more complex, the fighting man becomes less and less a man of muscle, and more and more a man of "nerve." Alexander, Cæsar and Napoleon would have stood a poor chance in personal combat against many of their followers. They led, because they were men of energy and cunning, able to maintain the subtle thing we call prestige.

Now the world has moved into an industrial era, and who are the great men of our time, the men whose lightest words are heeded, whose doings are spread upon the front pages of our newspapers? Obviously, they are the men of money. We may pretend to ourselves that we do not really stand in awe of a Morgan or a Rockefeller, but that we admire, let us say, an Edison or a Roosevelt. But Edison himself is a man of money, and will tell you that he had to be a man of money in order to be free to conduct his experiments. As for our politicians and statesmen, they either serve the men of money, or the men of money suppress them, as they did Roosevelt. The Morgans and the Rockefellers do not do much talking; they do not have to. They content themselves with being obeyed, and the shaping of our society is in their hands.

And yet, some of us really believe that there are higher faculties in man than the ability to manipulate the stock market. We consider that the great inventor, the great poet, the great moralist, contributes more to human happiness than the man who, by cunning and persistence, succeeds in monopolizing some material necessity of human life. "Poets," says Shelley, "are the unacknowledged legislators of mankind." If this strange statement is anywhere near to truth, it is surely of importance that we should decide what are the higher powers in men, and how they may be recognized, and how fostered and developed.

What is, in its essence, the process of evolution from the lower to the higher forms of mental life? It is a process of expanding consciousness; the developing of ability to apprehend a wider and wider circle of existence, to share it, to struggle for it as we do for the life we call our "own." The test of the higher mental forms is therefore a test of universality, of sympathetic inclusiveness; or, to use commoner words, it is a test of enlightened unselfishness.

Every human individual has the will to life, the instinct of self-preservation, which persuades him that he is of importance; but the test of his development is his ability to realize that, important though he may be, he is but a small part of the universe, and his highest interests are not in himself alone, his highest duties are not owed to himself alone. And as the life becomes more of the intellect, this fact becomes more and more obvious, more and more dominating. Men who monopolize the material things of the world and their control are necessarily self-seeking; but in the realm of the higher faculties this element, in the very nature of the case, is forced into the background. It is evident that truth is not truth for the Standard Oil Company, nor for J. P. Morgan and Company, nor yet for the government of the United States; it is truth for the whole of mankind, and one who sincerely labors for the truth does so for the universal benefit.

There may be, of course, an element of selfishness in the activities of poets and inventors. They may be seeking for fame; they may be hoping to make money out of their discoveries; but the greatest men we know have been dominated by an overwhelming impulse of creation, and when we read their lives, and discover in them signs of petty vanity or jealousy or greed, we are pained and shocked. What touches us most deeply is some mark of self-consecration and humility; as, for example, when Newton tells us that after all his life's labors he felt himself as a little child gathering sea-shells on the shore of the great ocean of truth; or when Alfred Russel Wallace, discovering that Darwin had been working longer than himself over the theory of the origin of species, generously withdrew and permitted the theory to go to the world in Darwin's name.

There are three faculties in man, usually described as intellect, feeling and will. According as one or the other faculty predominates, we have a great scientist, a great poet, or a great moralist. We might choose a representative of each type—let us say Newton, Shakespeare and Jesus—and spend much time in controversy as to which of the three types is the greatest, which makes the greatest contribution to human happiness. But it will suffice here to point out that the three faculties do not exclude one another; every man must have all three, and a perfectly rounded man should seek to develop all three. Jesus was considerable of a poet, and we should pay far less heed to Shakespeare if he had not been a moralist. Also there have been instances of great poets and painters who were scientists—for example, Leonardo and Goethe.

The fundamental difference between the scientist and the poet is that one is exploring nature and discovering things which actually exist, whereas the other is creating new life out of his own spirit. But the poet will find that his creations take but little hold upon life, if they are not guided and shaped by a deep understanding of life's fundamental nature and needs—in other words, if the poet is not something of a scientist. And in the same way, the very greatest discoveries of science seem to us like leaps of creative imagination; as if the mind had completed nature, through some intuitive and sympathetic understanding of what nature wished to be.

The point about these higher forms of human activity is that they renew and multiply life. We may say that if Jesus had never lived, others would have embodied and set forth with equal poignancy the revolutionary idea of the equality of all men as children of one common father. And perhaps this is true; but we have no way of being sure that it is true, and as we look back upon the last nineteen hundred years of human history, we are unable to imagine just what the life of mankind during those centuries would have been if Jesus had died when he was a baby. We do not know what modern thought might have been without Kant, or what modern music might have been without Beethoven. We are forced to admit that if it had not been for the patient wisdom and persuasive kindness of Lincoln, the Slave Power might have won its independence, and America today might have been a military camp like Europe, and the lives and thoughts of every one of us would have been different.

Or take the activities of the poet. Many years ago the writer was asked to name the men who had exercised the greatest influence upon him, and after much thought he named three: Jesus, Hamlet and Shelley. And now consider the significance of this reply. One of these people, Shelley, was what we call a "real" person; that is, a man who actually lived and walked upon the earth. Concerning Hamlet, it is believed there was once a Prince of Denmark by that name, but the character who is known to us as Hamlet is the creation of a poet's brain. As to the third figure, Jesus, the authorities dispute. Some say that he was a man who actually lived; others believe that he was God on earth; yet others, very learned, maintain that he is a legendary name around which a number of traditions have gathered.

To me it does not make a particle of difference which of the three possibilities happens to be true about Jesus. If he was God on earth, he was God in human form, under human limitations, and in that sense we are all gods on earth. And whether he really lived, or whether some poet invented him, matters not a particle so far as concerns his effect upon others. The emotions which moved him, the loves, the griefs, the high resolves, existed in the soul of someone, whether his name were Jesus or John; and these emotions have been recorded in such form that they communicate themselves to us, they become a part of our souls, they make us something different from what we were before we encountered them.

In other words, the poet makes in his own soul a new life, and then projects it into the world, and it becomes a force which makes over the lives of millions of other people. If you read the vast mass of criticism which has grown up about the figure of Hamlet, you learn that Hamlet is the type of the "modern man." Shakespeare was able to divine what the modern man would be; or perhaps we can go farther and say that Shakespeare helped to make the modern man what he is; the modern man is more of Hamlet, because he has taken Hamlet to his heart and pondered over Hamlet's problem. Or take Don Quixote. No doubt the follies of the "age of chivalry" would have died out of men's hearts in the end; but how much sooner they died because of the laughter of Cervantes! Or take "Les Miserables." Our prison system is not ideal by any means, but it is far less cruel than it was half a century ago, and we owe this in part to Victor Hugo. Every convict in the world is to some degree a happier man because of this vision which was projected upon the world from the soul of one great poet. No one can estimate the part which the writings of Tolstoi have played in the present revolution in Russia, but this we may say with certainty: there is not one man, woman or child in Russia at the present moment who is quite the same as he would have been if "Resurrection" had never been written.

In discussing the highest faculties of man we have so far refrained from using the word "genius." It is a word which has been cheapened by misuse, but we are now in position to use it. The things which we have just been considering are the phenomena of genius—and we can say this, even though we may not know exactly what genius is. Perhaps it is, as Frederic Myers asserts, a "subliminal uprush," the welling up into the consciousness of some part of the content of the subconscious mind. Or perhaps it is something of what man calls "divine." Or perhaps it is the first dawning, the first hint of that super-race which will some day replace mankind. Perhaps we are witnessing the same thing that happened on the earth when glimmerings of reason first broke upon the mind of some poor, bewildered ape. We cannot be sure; but this much we can say: the man of genius represents the highest activity of the mind of which we as yet have knowledge. He represents the spirit of man, fully emancipated, fully conscious, and taking up the task of creation; taking human life as raw material, and making it over into something more subtle, more intense, more significant, more universal than it ever was before, or ever would have been without the intervention of this new God-man.

CHAPTER X

MYSELF AND MY NEIGHBOR

(Compares the new morality with the old, and discusses the relative importance of our various duties.)

So now we may say that we know what are the great and important things in life. Slowly and patiently, with infinite distress and waste and failure, but yet inevitably, the life of man is being made over and multiplied to infinity, by the power of the thinking mind, impelled by the joy and thrill of the creative action, and guided by the sense of responsibility, the instinct to serve, which we call conscience. To develop these higher faculties is the task we have before us, and the supreme act to which we dedicate ourselves.

So now we are in position to define the word moral. Assuming that our argument be accepted, that action is moral which tends to foster the best and highest forms of life we know, and to aid them in developing their highest powers; that is immoral which tends to destroy the best life we know, or to hinder its rapid development.

Let us now proceed to apply these tests to the practices of man; first as an individual, and then as a social being. What are my duties to myself, and what are my duties to the world about me?

You will note that these questions differ somewhat from those of the old morality. Jesus told us, first, that we should love the Lord our God, and, second, that we should love our neighbor as ourself. Some would say that modern thought has dismissed God from consideration; but I would prefer to say that modern thought has decided that the place where we encounter God most immediately is in our own miraculously expanding consciousness. Our duty toward God is our duty to make of ourselves the most perfect product of the Divine Incarnation that we can become. Our duty to our neighbor is to help him to do the same.

Of course, as we come to apply these formulas, we find that they overlap and mingle inextricably; the two duties are really one duty looked at from different points of view. We decide that we owe it to ourselves to develop our best powers of thinking, and we discover that in so doing we make ourselves better fitted to live as citizens, better equipped to help our fellow men. We go out into our city to serve others by making the city clean and decent, and we find that we have helped to save ourselves from a pestilence.

The most commonly accepted, or at any rate the most commonly preached, of all formulas is the "golden rule," "Do unto others as you would have them do unto you." This formula is good so far as it goes, but you note that it leaves undetermined the all-important question, what *ought* we to want others to do unto us. If I am an untrained child, what I would have others do unto me is to give me plenty of candy; therefore, under the golden rule, my highest duty becomes to distribute free candy to the world. The "golden rule" is obviously consistent with all forms of self-indulgence, and with all forms of stagnation; it might result in a civilization more static than China.

Or let us take the formula which the German philosopher Kant worked out as the final product of his thinking: "Act so that you would be willing for your action to become a general rule of conduct." Here again is the same problem. There are many possible general rules of conduct. Some would prefer one, some others; and there is no possible way of escape from the fact that before men can agree what to do, they must decide what they wish to make of their lives.

To the formula of Jesus, "Thou shalt love thy neighbor as thyself," the answer is obvious enough: "Suppose my neighbor is not worthy of as much love as myself?" To be sure, it is a perilous thing for me to have to decide this question; nevertheless, it may be a fact that I am a great inventor, and that my neighbor is a sexual pervert. There is, of course, a sense in which I may love him, even so; I may love the deeper possibilities of his nature, which religious ecstasy can appeal to and arouse. But in spite of all ecstasies and all efforts, it may be that his disease—physical, mental and moral—has progressed to such a point that it is necessary to confine him, or to castrate him, or even to asphyxiate him painlessly. To say that I must love such a man as myself is, to say the least, to be vague. We can see how the indiscriminate preaching of such a formula would open the flood-gates of sentimentality and fraud.

Modern thinking says: Thou shalt love the highest possibilities of life, and thou shalt labor diligently to foster them; moreover, because life is always growing, and new possibilities are forever dawning in the human spirit, thou shalt keep an open mind and an inquiring temper, and be ready at any time to begin life afresh.

Such is the formula. It is not simple; and when we come to apply it, we find that it constantly grows more complex. When we attempt to decide our duty to ourselves, we find that we have in us a number of different beings, each with separate and sometimes conflicting duties and needs. We have in us the physical man and the economic man, and these clamor for their rights, and must have at least a part of their rights, before we can go on to be the intellectual man, the moral man, or the artistic man. So our life becomes a series of compromises and adjustments between a thousand conflicting desires and duties; between the different beings which we might be, but can be only to a certain extent, and at certain times. We shall see, as we come to investigate one field after another of human activity, that we never have an absolute certainty, never an absolute right, never an absolute duty; never can we shut our eyes, and go blindly ahead upon one course of action, to the exclusion of every other consideration! On the contrary, we sit in the seat of self-determination as a highly trained and skillful engineer. We keep our eyes upon a dozen different gauges; we press a lever here and touch a regulator there; we decide that now is a time for speed, and now for caution; and knowing all the time that the safety, not merely of ourselves, but of many passengers, depends upon the decisions of each moment.

CHAPTER XI

THE MIND AND THE BODY

(Discusses the interaction between physical and mental things, and the possibility of freedom in a world of fixed causes.)

It is our plan, so far as possible, to discuss the problems of the mind in one section of this book, and the problems of the body in another; but just as we found that we could not separate our duties to ourself from our duties to our neighbors, so we find that the mind and the body are inextricably interwoven, and that whenever we probe deeply into one, we discover the other. The interaction of the mind and the body is a fascinating problem into which we must look for a moment, not because we expect to solve it, but because it illuminates the whole subject.

The human body is a machine. It takes in carbon and oxygen, and burns them, and gives out carbon dioxide and other waste products, and develops energy in proportion to the amount of carbon it consumes. This machine has its elaborate apparatus of action and reaction, its sensory organs where outside stimuli are received, its nerves like telegraph wires to carry these impressions, its brain cells to store them and to transform them into reactions. We know to some extent how these brain cells work. We know what portions of the brain are devoted to this or that activity. We know that if we stick a pin into a certain spot we shall paralyze the left forefinger. We know that by injecting a certain drug, or by breathing a certain gas, we can cause this or that sensation or reaction, such as laughing or weeping or mania. We know what poisons are generated in the system by anger, and what chemical changes take place in a muscle that is tired. All this is part of a vast new science which is called bio-chemistry, or the chemistry of life.

Our bodies, therefore, are part of the material universe, and subject to the laws or ways of being of this universe. The first of these laws that we know is the law of causation. Every change in the universe has its cause, and that in turn had another cause; this chain is never broken, no matter how far we go, and the same causes universally produce the same effects. If you see a ball move on a billiard table, you know that the ball did not move itself; you know that something struck the ball or tilted the table. You discover that the motion of the ball moves the air around it, and the waves of that motion are spread through the room. They strike the walls, and the motion is carried on through the walls, and if we had instruments sensitive enough, we could feel the motion of that billiard ball at the other side of the world, and a few million years from now at the most remote of the stars. This is what is called the law of the conservation of energy, and when we discover something like radium which seems to violate that law by giving out unlimited quantities of energy, we investigate and discover a new form of energy locked up in the atom. In the disintegration of the atom we have a source of power which, when we have learned to use it, will multiply perhaps millions of times the powers we are now able to use on this earth. But energy, no matter how many times it is transformed, and in what strange ways it reappears, always remains, and is never destroyed, and never created out of nothing.

My friend the great physiologist once took me into his laboratory and showed me a little aquarium in which some minute creatures were wiggling about—young sea-urchins, if I remember. The physiologist took a bottle containing some chemical, and dropped a single drop into the water, and instantly all these little black creatures, which had been darting aimlessly in every direction through the water, turned and swam all in one direction, toward the light. They swam until they touched the walls of the aquarium, and there they stuck, trying their best to swim farther. "And now," said my friend, "that is what we call a 'tropism,' and all life is a tropism. What you see in that aquarium means that some day we shall know just what combination of chemicals causes a human being to move this way or that, to do this thing or that. When bio-chemistry has progressed sufficiently, we shall be able to make human qualities, perhaps in the sperm, perhaps in the embryo, perhaps day by day by means of diet or injection."

Said I: "Some day, when bio-chemistry has progressed far enough, you will know what combination of chemicals causes a man to vote the Democratic or Republican ticket."

"Why not?" answered my friend. (He has a sense of humor about all things except this sacred bio-chemistry.)

Said I: "When you have got to that stage, keep the secret carefully, and we will fix up a scheme, and a few days before election we will release some gas in our big cities, and sweep the country for the Socialist ticket."

But jesting aside: if the human body is a material thing, existing in the material world and subject to causation, there must be material reasons for the actions of human bodies, just the same as for the moving of billiard balls. We hear the sound of a billiard ball striking the cushion, and we are prepared to accept the idea that the thing we call hearing in us is caused by the impinging of sound waves upon our eardrums. And if we investigate human beings in the mass, we find every reason to believe that they act according to laws, and that there are material causes for their acts. If you get up and shout fire in a theater, you know how the audience will behave. If you study statistics, you can say that in any large city a certain fixed number of human beings are going to commit suicide every month; you can even say that more are going to commit suicide in the month of June than in any other month. You can say that more people are going to die at two o'clock in the morning than at any other hour. You know that certain changes in the weather will cause all human beings to behave in the same way. You know that an increase of prices or an increase of unemployment will cause a certain additional number of men to commit crimes, and a certain additional number of women to become prostitutes. You know that if a man overeats, his thoughts will change their color; he will have what he calls "the blues." I might cite a thousand other illustrations to prove that human minds are subject to material laws, and therefore to investigation by the bio-chemists.

But now, stop a moment. Here you sit reading a book. Something in the book pleases you, and you say, "Good!" Perhaps you slap your knee or clench your fist. Now here is a motion of your hand, which stirs the air about you, and which, according to the laws of energy, will spread its effects to the other side of the world, and even to the farthest of the stars. Or perhaps the book makes you angry, and you throw it down in disgust; an entirely different motion, which will affect the other side of the world and the farthest of the stars in an entirely different way. The machine of the universe will be forever altered because of that slapping of your knee or that throwing down of your book.

And what was the cause of these things? So far as we can see, the material cause was exactly the same in each case—the reading of certain letters. Two human beings, sitting side by side and reading exactly the same letters, might be affected in exactly opposite ways. It seems hardly rational to maintain that the material difference of two pairs of eyes, moving over exactly the same set of letters, could have resulted in two such different motions of the hands. As a matter of fact, the very same letters may affect the same person in different ways. The composer, Edward MacDowell, once told me how on his birthday his pupils sent him a gift, with a card containing some lines from the opera "Rheingold," beginning, "O singe fort"—that is, "Oh, sing on." But the composer happened, when glancing at the card, to think French instead of German, and got the message, "Oh, powerful monkey!" This, of course, was disconcerting to a famous piano performer, and his pupils, if they had been watching his face, would have seen an unexpected reaction. It seems manifest, does it not, that the cause of this difference of reaction was not any difference of the letters, but purely a difference of *thought*? So it appears that thoughts may change the material universe; they may break the chain of causation, and interfere with material events.

Compare the two things, a state of consciousness and say, a steam shovel. They are entirely different, and so far as we can see, entirely incompatible and unrelated. Can anyone imagine how a thought can turn into a steam shovel, or a steam shovel into a thought? We can understand how a steam shovel lifts a mass of earth out of the ground, and we can understand how a human hand moves a lever which causes the shovel to act; but we are unable to conceive how a state of mind—whether it be a desire for pay, or an ideal of service, or a vision of the Panama Canal—can so affect a steam shovel as to cause it to move. We can sit and think motion at a billiard ball for a thousand years, and it does not move; but when we think motion at our hand, it moves instantly, and passes on the motion to the billiard ball or the steam shovel. When fire touches our hand it sends some kind of vibration to the brain, and in some inconceivable way that vibration is turned into a state of consciousness called pain, and that is turned, "as quick as thought," into another kind of motion, the jerking back of our hand.

So it seems certain that consciousness really does "butt in" on the chain of natural causation. And yet, just see in what position this leaves the scientist who is investigating life! Imagine if you can, the plight of a doctor who wanted to prescribe a diet for a sick person, if he knew that every piece of chicken and every piece of fish were free to decide of its own impulse whether or not it would be digested in the human stomach. But the plight of this doctor would be nothing to the plight of the chemist or the biologist or the engineer who was asked to do his thinking and his planning in a world containing a billion and a quarter human beings, each one a lawless agent, each one a source of new and unforeseeable energies, each one acting as a "first cause," and starting new chains of activity, tearing the universe to pieces according to his own whims. What kind of a universe would that be? It would simply be a chaos; there could be no thinking, there could be no life in it; there could be no two things the same in it, and no laws of any sort.

So then we fall back into the hands of the "determinists," who assert one unbreakable chain of natural causation, and regard the human body as an automaton. We go back to the bio-chemist, who purposes some day to ascertain for us just exactly what molecules of matter in just what positions and combinations in the brain cells of William Shakespeare caused him to perpetrate a mixed metaphor. We go back to the belief that human beings act as they must act, because the clock of life, wound up and started, must move in such and such a fashion.

But now, let us see what are the implications of that theory! Here am I writing a book, appealing to men to act in certain ways. Of course, I know that not all will follow my advice. Some will be foolish—or what seems to me foolish. Others will be weak, and will resolve to act in certain ways, and then go and act in other ways. But some will be just; some will be free; some will use their brains—because, you see, I am convinced that they *can* use their brains! I am convinced that ideas will affect and stir them, in complete defiance of the bio-chemist, who tells me that they act that way because of certain chemicals in their brain cells, and that I write my book because of other chemicals, and that my idea that I am writing the book because I want to write it is a delusion, and that the whole thing is happening just so because the universe was wound up that way.

Now, this an unsolved problem, and I have no solution to offer. What I have set forth is in substance one of the four "antinomies" of Kant, and you can see for yourself how it is possible to prove either side, and impossible to be sure of either. Perhaps there is really a duality in life. Perhaps there are two aspects of the universe, the material and the spiritual, and perhaps they do not really interact as they seem to, but both are guided and determined by some higher reality of life of which we know nothing. In that case there would really be a chemical equivalent for every thought, and there would be a trace of consciousness for every material atom in the universe. Maybe the theologians are right, and in the universal consciousness of God the whole future exists predetermined. Maybe to God there is no such thing as time; the past, the present, and the future are all alike to Him.

There is nothing more painful to the human mind than to have to confess its own impotence. Yet I can see no escape from the dilemma we are here facing. There is not a man alive who does not assume the freedom of the will, who does not show in all his acts that he agrees with old Dr. Samuel Johnson: "We know we are free and there's an end on't." Without a belief in freedom we cannot get beyond the animal, we cannot become the masters of our own souls. And yet, the man who swallows that idea whole, and goes out into the world and preaches personal morality to the neglect of the fundamental economic facts, the facts of the body in its relationship to all other bodies—we know what happens to that man; he becomes a shouting fool. Unless he is literally a fool, or a knave, he quickly discovers his own futility, and proceeds to use his common sense, in spite of all his theories. "Come to Jesus!" cried William Booth, and he went out in the streets of London to save souls with a bass drum; but presently, in day by day contact with the degradation of the London slums, he realized that he could not save souls so long as those souls were dwelling in starved and lousy bodies. So William Booth with his Salvation Army took to starting night shelters and cast-off clothing bureaus!

And of exactly the same sort is the bewilderment which falls to the lot of the scientist who is honest and willing to face the facts. The bio-chemist with his test tubes and his microscopes and his complex apparatus of research sits himself down and accumulates a mass of information about the human body. He investigates the diseases of the body and learns in detail just how these diseases spread and sometimes how they are caused; he can present you with a diagnosis, showing the exact stage to which the degeneration of a certain organ has proceeded, and perhaps he can suggest to you a change of diet or some drug which will, for a time at least, check the process of the breakdown. But in other cases he will be perfectly helpless; he will be, as it were, buried under the mass of detail which he has accumulated; he will find the vital energy depressed, and he will not know any way to renew it. But along will come some mental specialist, who in a half hour's talk with the patient, by a simple change in the patient's *ideas*, will completely make over the patient's life, and set going a new vital process which will restore the body to its former health. A religious enthusiast may do this, a psychotherapist may do it, a moral genius may do it; and the physician with all his learning will find himself like a man on the outside of a house, peering in through the windows and trying in vain to find out something about the life of the family and its guests.

This is humiliating to the chemist and the medical man, but they have to face it, because it is a fact. In the seat of authority over the human body there sits a higher being which, without any religious implications, we may call the soul; or, if it is impossible to get away from the religious implication of that word, we will call it the consciousness, or the personality. This master of the house of life is in many ways dependent upon the house. If the furnace goes out he freezes, and if the house takes fire and burns up—well, he disappears and leaves no address. But in other ways the master of the house is really master, and is a worker of miracles. He does things which we do not at all understand, and cannot yet even foresee, but which often completely make the house over.

William James, a scientist of real authority, has a wonderful essay, "The Powers of Men," in which he sets forth the fact that human beings as a general rule make use of only a small portion of the energies which dwell in their beings, and that one of our problems is to find the ways by which we can draw upon stores of hidden energy which we have within us. Also, in a fascinating book, "Varieties of the Religious Experience," James has endeavored to study and analyze the phenomena which hitherto the physician and the biologist have been disposed to ridicule and neglect. But unless I am mistaken, every scientist in the end will be forced to come back to the central fact, that life is a unity, and that the heart of it is the spirit; that what we call the will is not an accident, not a delusion, not some by-product of nature, but is the very secret of life; and that behind it is a vast ocean of power, which now and then sweeps away all dykes, and floods into the human consciousness.

The writer of this book is now a patient and plodding teacher of a certain economic doctrine, a preacher of what he might call anti-parasitism. He has come to the conclusion that the habit of men to enslave their fellows and exploit them and draw their substance from them without return—that this habit is destructive to all civilization, and is incompatible with any of the higher forms of life, intellectual, moral or artistic. He has come to the conclusion that there is no use attempting to build a structure of social life until there is a sound foundation; in other words, until the capitalist system has been replaced by cooperation. But in his youth he was, or thought he was, a poet, and touched upon that strange and wonderful thing which we call genius. He saw his own consciousness, as it were a leaf driven before a mighty tempest of spiritual energy. And he believes that this experience was no delusion, but was a revelation of the hidden mysteries of being. He still has memories of this startling experience, still hints of it in his consciousness; something still leaps in his memory, like a race-horse, or like the war-horse of Revelations, which "scenteth the battle afar off, the thunder of the captains and the shouting." Because of these things he can never accept any philosophy which shackles the human spirit, he will never in his thought attempt to set bounds to the possibilities of human life. The very heart of life beats in us, the wonder of it and the glory of it swells like a tide behind us. New universes are born in us, or, if you prefer, they are made by us; and the process is one of endless joy, of rapture beyond anything that the average man can at present imagine, or that any instruments invented by science can weigh or measure.

CHAPTER XII

THE MIND OF THE BODY

(Discusses the subconscious mind, what it is, what it does to the body, and how it can be controlled and made use of by the intelligence.)

The importance of the mind in matters of health becomes clearer when we understand that what we commonly call our minds—the mental states which confront us day by day in our consciousness—are really but a small portion of our total mind. In addition to this conscious mind there is an enormous mass of our personality which is like a storehouse attached to our dwelling, a place to which we do not often go, but to which we can go in case of need. This storehouse is our memory, the things we know and can recall at will. And then there is another, still vaster storehouse—no one has ever measured or guessed the size of it—which apparently contains everything that we have ever known, perhaps also everything that our ancestors have known. A common simile for the human mind is that of an iceberg; a certain portion of it appears above the surface of the sea, but there is seven times as much of it floating out of sight under the water.

This subconscious mind seems to be the portion most closely united with the body. It has its seat in the back parts of the brain, in the spinal cord and the greater nervous ganglia, such as the solar plexus. It is the portion of our mind which controls the activities of our body, all those miraculous things which went on before we first opened our eyes to the light, and which go on while we sleep, and never cease until we die. When we cut our finger and admit foreign germs to our blood, some mysterious power causes millions of our blood corpuscles to be rushed to this spot, to destroy and devour the invading enemy. We do not know how this is done, but it is an intelligent act, measured and precisely regulated, as much so as a railroad time-table. When the supply of nourishment in the body becomes low, something issues a notice by way of our stomach, which we call hunger; when we take food into the stomach, something pours out the gastric juice to digest it; when this digested food is prepared and taken up in the blood stream, something decides what portion of it shall be turned into muscle, what into brain cells, what into hair, what into finger nails. Sometimes, of course, mistakes are made and we have diseases. But for the most part all this infinitely intricate process goes on day and night without a hitch, and it is all the work of what we might call "the mind of the body."

And just as our material bodies are the product of an age-long process of development repeated in embryo by every individual, so is this mental life a product of long development, and carries memories of this far-off process. In our instincts there dwells all the past, not merely of the human race, but of all life, and if we should ever succeed in completely probing the subconscious mind and bringing it into our consciousness, it would be the same as if we were free to ramble about in all the past. Huxley set forth the fact that all the history of evolution is told in a piece of chalk; and we probably do not exaggerate in saying that all the history of the universe is in the subconscious mind of every human being. When the partridge which has just come out of the egg sees the shadow of the hawk flit by and crouches motionless as a leaf, the partridge is not acting upon any knowledge which it has acquired in the few minutes since it was hatched. It is acting upon a knowledge impressed upon its subconscious mind by the experience of millions of partridges, perhaps for tens of thousands of years. When the physician lifts the newly born infant by its ankle and spanks it to make it cry, the physician is using his conscious reason, because he has learned from previous experience, or has been taught in the schools that it is necessary for the child's breathing apparatus to be instantly cleared. But when the child responds to the spanking with a yell, it is not moved by reasoned indignation at an undeserved injury; it is following an automatic reaction, as a result of the experience of infants in the stone age, experience which in some obscure way has been registered and stored in the infant cerebellum.

Science is now groping its way through this underworld of thought. Obviously we should have here a most powerful means of influencing the body, if by any chance we could control it. We are continually seeking in medical and surgical ways to stimulate or to retard activities of the body, which are controlled entirely by this subconscious mind. If we are suffering intense pain in a joint, we put on a mustard plaster, what we call a counter-irritant, to trouble the skin and draw the congested blood away from the place of the pain. On the other hand, we may stimulate the functions of the intestines by the application of hot fomentations, to bring the blood more actively to that region. But if by any means we could make clear our wishes to the subconscious mind, we should be dealing with headquarters, and should get quicker and more permanent results.

Can we by any possibility do this? To begin with, let me tell you of a simple experiment that I have witnessed. I once knew a man who had learned to control the circulation of his blood by his conscious will. I have seen him lay his two hands on the table, both of the same color, and without moving the hands, cause one hand to turn red and the other to turn pale. And, obviously, so far as this man is concerned, the problem of counter-irritants has been solved. He is a mental mustard plaster.

And what was done by this man's own will can be done to others in many ways. The most obvious is a device which we call hypnotism. This is a kind of sleep which affects only the conscious control of the body, but leaves all the senses awake. In this hypnotic sleep or "trance" we discover that the subconscious mind is a good deal like the Henry Dubb of the Socialist cartoons; it is faithful and persistent, very strong in its own limited field, but comically credulous, willing to believe anything that is told it, and to take orders from any one who climbs into the seat of authority. You have perhaps attended one of the exhibitions which traveling hypnotists are accustomed to give in country villages. You have seen some bumpkin brought upon the stage and hypnotized, and told that he is in the water and must swim for his life, or that he is in the midst of a hornets' nest, or that his trousers are torn in the seat—any comical thing that will cause an audience to howl with laughter.

These facts were first discovered nearly a hundred and fifty years ago by a French doctor named Mesmer. He was a good deal of a charlatan, and would not reveal his secrets, and probably the scientific men of that time were glad to despise him, because what he did was so new and strange. There is a certain type of scientific mind which sits aloft on a throne with a framed diploma above its head, and says that what it knows is science and what it does not know is nonsense. And so "mesmerism" was left for the quacks and traveling showmen. But half a century later a French physician named Liébault took up this method of hypnotism, without all the fakery that had been attached to it. He experimented and discovered that he could cure not merely phobias and manias, fixed ideas, hysterias and melancholias; he could cure definite physical diseases of the physical body, such as headache, rheumatism, and hemorrhage. Later on two other physicians, Janet and Charcot, developed definite schools of "psychotherapy." They rejected hypnotism as in most cases too dangerous, but used a milder form which is known as "hypnoidization." You would be surprised to know how many ailments which baffle the skill of medical men and surgeons yield completely to a single brief treatment by such a mental specialist.

All that is necessary is some method to tap the subconscious mind. In many cases the subconsciousness knows what is the matter, and will tell at once—a secret that is completely hidden from the consciousness. For example, a man's hands shake; they have been shaking for years, and he has no idea why, but his subconscious mind explains that they first began to shake with grief over the death of his wife; also, the subconscious mind meekly and instantly accepts the suggestion that the time for grief is past, and that the hands will never shake again.

Or here is a woman who has become convinced that worms are crawling all over her. Everything that touches her becomes a worm, even the wrinkles in her dress are worms, and she is wild with nervousness, and of course is on the way to the lunatic asylum. She is hypnotized and sees the operator catching these worms one by one and killing them. She is told that he has killed the last, but she insists, "No, there is one more." The operator clutches that one, and she is perfectly satisfied, and completely cured. Her husband writes, expressing his relief that he no longer has to "sleep every night in a fish pond." This instance with many others is told by Professor Quackenbos in his book, "Hypnotic Therapeutics."

Among the most powerful means to influence the subconscious personality is religious excitement. Religion has come down to us from ancient times, and its fears and ecstasies are a part of our instinctive endowment. Those who can sway religious emotions can cure disease, not merely fixed ideas, but many diseases which appear to be entirely physical, but which psycho-analysis reveals to be hysterical in nature. Of course these religious persons who heal by laying on of hands or by purely mental means deny indignantly that they are using hypnotism or anything like it. I am aware that I shall bring upon myself a flood of letters from Christian Scientists if I identify their methods of curing with "animal magnetism" and "manipulation," and other devices of the devil which they repudiate. All I can say is that their miracles are brought about by affecting the subconscious mind; there is no other way to bring them about, and for my part I cannot see that it makes a great difference whether the subconscious mind is affected by a hand laid on the forehead, or by a hand waved in the air, or by an incantation pronounced, or by a prayer thought in silence. If you can persuade the subconscious mind that God is operating upon it, that God is omnipotent and is directing this particular healing, that is the most powerful suggestion imaginable, and is the basis of many cures. But if in order to achieve this, it is necessary for me to persuade myself that I can find some meaning in the metaphysical moonshine of Mother Eddy—why, then, I am very sorry, but I really prefer to remain sick.

But such is not the case. You do not have to believe anything that is not true; you simply have to understand the machinery of the subconscious, and how to operate it. We are only beginning to acquire that knowledge, and we need an open mind, free both from the dogmatism of the medical men and the fanaticism of the "faith curists." A few years ago in London I met a number of people who were experimenting in an entirely open-minded way with mental healing, and I was interested in their ideas. I happened to be traveling on the Continent, and on the train my wife was seized by a very dreadful headache. She was lying with her head in my lap, suffering acutely, and I thought I would try an experiment, so I put my hand upon her forehead, without telling her what I was doing, and concentrated my attention with the greatest possible intensity upon her headache. I had an idea of the cause of it; I understood that headaches are caused by the irritation of the sensory nerves of the brain by fatigue poisons, or other waste matter which the blood has not been able to eliminate. I formed in my mind a vivid picture of what the blood would have to do to relieve that headache, and I concentrated my mental energies upon the command to her subconscious mind that it should perform these particular functions. In a few minutes my wife sat up with a look of great surprise on her face and said, "Why, my headache is gone! It went all at once!"

That, of course, might have been a coincidence; but I tried the experiment many times, and it happened over and over. On another occasion I was able to cure the pain of an ulcerated tooth; I was able to cure it half a dozen times, but never permanently, it always returned, and finally the tooth had to come out. My wife experimented with me in the same way, and found that she was able to cure an attack of dyspepsia; but, curiously enough, she at once gave herself a case of dyspepsia—something she had never known in her life before. So now I will not allow her to experiment with me, and she will not allow me to experiment with her! But we are quite sure that people with psychic gifts can definitely affect the subconscious mind of others by purely mental means. We are prepared to believe in the miracles of the New Testament, and in the wonders of Lourdes, as well as in the healings of the Christian Scientists and the New Thoughters, which cannot be disputed by any one who is willing to take the trouble to investigate. We can face these facts without losing our reason, without ceasing to believe that everything in life has a cause, and that we can find out this cause if we investigate thoroughly.

CHAPTER XIII

EXPLORING THE SUBCONSCIOUS

(Discusses automatic writing, the analysis of dreams, and other methods by which a whole new universe of life has been brought to human knowledge.)

One of the most common methods of exploring the subconscious mind is the method of automatic writing. I have never tried this myself, but tens of thousands of people are sitting every night with a "ouija" in front of them, holding a pencil on a piece of paper and letting their subconscious minds write what they please. Most of them are hoping to get messages from the dead—a problem which we shall discuss in the next chapter. Suffice it for the moment to say that automatic writing and table rapping and other devices of mediumship have opened up to us a vast mass of subconscious mentality. A part of the scientific world still takes a contemptuous attitude and calls this all humbug, but many of our greatest scientists have been persuaded to investigate, and have become convinced that in this mass of subconsciousness there is mingled, not merely the mind of the medium, but the minds of all those present, and possibly other minds as well. For my part, I do not see how any one can study disinterestedly the proceedings of the Society for Psychical Research and not become convinced that telepathy at least is one of the powers of the subconscious mind.

Telepathy is what is popularly known as "thought transmission." Every one must know people who are what is called "psychic," and will know what is happening to some friend in another part of the world, or will go upstairs because they "sense" that some one wants them, or will go to the door because they "have a hunch" that some one is coming. And maybe these things are only chance, but you will be unscientific if you do not take the trouble to read and learn what modern investigators have brought out on such subjects.

This much is certain, and is denied by no competent investigator: whatever has been in your mind is there still, and it is possible to find a way of tapping the buried memory. An old woman, delirious with fever, begins to babble in a strange language, and it is discovered that she is talking ancient Hebrew. The woman is entirely illiterate, and her conscious memory knows no language but her own, her conscious mind has no ideas beyond those of her domestic life and the gossip of the village. But investigation is made, and it is discovered that when this woman was a girl, she worked in the home of a Hebrew scholar, and heard him reading aloud. She did not understand a word of what she heard, and was not consciously listening to it; nevertheless, every syllable of it had been stored away forever by her subconscious mind. Innumerable cases of this sort have been established; and, as a matter of fact, we might have been prepared for such discoveries by the memory-feats of the conscious mind. It is well known that Mozart, when a child, could listen to a new opera, and go home and play it over note for note. At present there is a child in America, giving exhibitions in public, carrying on thirty games of chess at the same time. There have been others who do sums of mental arithmetic, such as multiplying thirty-two figures by thirty-two figures, or reciting the Bible backwards.

All this seems incredible; and yet there is something still more incredible. Suppose that these same powers, which are stored in our subconscious minds, were stored also in the minds of animals! A few years ago Maurice Maeterlinck published a book, "The Unknown Guest," in the course of which he tells about his experiments with the so-called Elberfeld horses: two animals which had been trained for years by their owner to give signals by moving their forefeet, and which apparently could count and divide and multiply large sums, and extract square and cube root, and spell out names, and recognize sounds, scents and colors, and read time from the face of a watch. Of course, it is easy to say that this is absurd, that the horses must have got some signals from their trainer; but, as it happened, they would do their work in the absence of their trainer; they would do it in the dark, or with a sack over their heads, and the best scientific minds of Germany were unable to suggest any test conditions which could not be met. There have been many gigantic frauds in the world, and this may have been one of them; on the other hand, there have been many new discoveries, and for my part I will finish exploring the miracles of the subconscious mind of man, before I presume to say that anything is impossible in the subconscious mind of a horse or a dog. Also I will wait for some learned person to explain to me how the subconscious minds of horses and dogs know enough to build and repair their bones and teeth, so cleverly that modern architectural and engineering science could teach them nothing. I ask, also, if it is possible to find a region in the subconsciousness which is common to two people, why is it absurd to suggest that there might be a region common to a man and a horse? Why is this any more absurd than that they should eat the same food and breathe the same air and feel the same affection and be frightened at the same dangers?

The only persons who will be dogmatic about such subjects are the persons who are ignorant. Those who take the trouble to investigate, discover more wonderful things every day, and they realize that we have here a whole universe of knowledge, to which we have as yet barely opened the doors. Consider, for example, the facts which we are acquiring on the subject of personality and what it means. You would say, perhaps, that if there is anything you know positively, it is that you are one person, and have never been anybody else, and that your body belongs to you, and that nobody else ever has used or ever can use it. But what would you say if I told you that tomorrow "you" might cease to be, and somebody else might be in possession of your body, walking it around and wearing its clothes and spending its money? What if I were to tell you that there might be in "you," or in your body, half a dozen different personalities which you have never known or dreamed of, and that tomorrow there might break out a war between them and "you," as to which of the half dozen people should hear with your ears and speak with your tongue and walk about with your clothes on? Unless you are familiar with the literature of multiple personality, you would surely say that this was unbelievable—quite as much so as a mathematical horse!

Let us begin with the case of the Reverend Ansel Bourne, who was many years ago a perfectly respectable clergyman in a Rhode Island town. One day he disappeared, and his family did not hear of him. A year or two later there was a store-keeper in a town in Pennsylvania, who suddenly came to himself as the Reverend Ansel Bourne, not knowing what he had been in the meantime, or how he came to be keeping a store. Under hypnotism it developed that he had in him two personalities, and his trance personality recollected all that had been happening in the meantime and told about it freely.

Or take the still more fascinating case of the young lady who is known in the literature of psychotherapy as Miss Beauchamp. Her story is told in a book, "The Dissociation of a Personality," by Dr. Morton Prince of Boston.

Some thirty years ago Miss Beauchamp, a very conscientious and dignified young lady, became nervous and ill, and took to doing strange things, which were a source of shame and humiliation to her. Under hypnotism it was discovered to be a case of multiple personality. The other personality, who finally gave herself the name of Sally, was entirely different in character from Miss Beauchamp, being mischievous, vain, and primitive as a child. She conceived an intense dislike for Miss Beauchamp, whom she called by abusive names; at times when she could get possession of Miss Beauchamp's body, she delighted in playing humiliating tricks upon her enemy, spending her money, running her into debt, breaking her engagements, disgracing her before her friends. Sally was always well and Miss Beauchamp was always ill, and Sally would take the body, for which they fought for possession, and take it for long and exhausting walks, and leave it cold and miserable, lost and penniless, in the possession of Miss Beauchamp! And of course this made Miss Beauchamp more and more a wreck, and Sally took possession of more and more of her time. Sally knew everything that Miss Beauchamp did and thought, but Miss Beauchamp did not know about Sally. She only knew that there were gaps in her life, during which she did things she could not explain. And because she did not want her friends to think her insane, she would try to hide this dreadful condition of affairs; but Sally would spoil her plans by writing letters to her friends, and also by writing insulting letters for Miss Beauchamp to find when she took possession again.

Then one day, after several years of treatment, there appeared yet another personality, who knew nothing about Miss Beauchamp or Sally either, and only knew what Miss Beauchamp had known up to some years before. Miss Beauchamp had a college education, and wrote and spoke French; Sally knew no French, and tried in vain to learn it; the new personality did not have a college education at all. Nevertheless, after long experiment, the story of which is as fascinating as any novel you ever read, Dr. Prince discovered that this was the real Miss Beauchamp; the others were "split off" personalities. He traced the cause to a severe mental shock, and succeeded in the end in combining the first Miss Beauchamp with the last, and in suppressing the obstinate and wanton Sally. As you read this story, you watch him mentally murdering a human being; "Sally" clamors pitifully for life, but he condemns her to death, and relentlessly executes his sentence. It is a "movie" thriller with a happy ending, and I should think it would make disconcerting reading to persons who believe that each of us is one immortal soul, or "has" one immortal soul, and is responsible for it to a personal God.

There is never any end to the problems of these multiple personalities, and each case is a test of the judgment and ingenuity of the specialist. He will try to make one personality "stick," and will fail, and will have to accept another, or a combination of two. In one case, he found that he could not get the right personality to "stick" except under hypnosis, so he decided to leave the man in a mild state of trance, and the new personality lived all the rest of its life in that condition. If you wish to know more about this subject you can find books in any well-equipped library. I mention one, "The Riddle of Personality," by H. Addington Bruce, because it contains in the appendix an excellent list of the literature of the subconscious in all its many aspects.

There is another, and most fascinating method of exploring this underworld of the mind, and that is the study of dreams. Some fifteen years ago a psychotherapist in New York told me about the discoveries of a physician in Vienna, and gave me some pamphlets, written in very difficult and technical German. Since then this Professor Freud has been translated, and has become a fad, and the absurdities of his followers make one a little apologetic for him. But we do not give up Jesus because of the torturers and bigots who call themselves Christians, and in the same way we have no right to blame Freud for all the absurdities of the psychoanalysts.

Probably there never was a time in human history when there were not people who interpreted dreams, and you can still buy "dream books" for twenty-five cents, and learn that a white horse means that you are going to get a letter from your sweetheart tomorrow; then you can buy another dream book, telling you that a white horse means there is going to be a death in your family within the year. Naturally this prejudices thinking people against dream analysis; yet, dreams are facts, and every fact has its cause, and if you dream about a white horse, there must assuredly be some reason for your dreaming this particular thing. Of course we know that if you eat mince-pie and welsh-rabbit at midnight, you will dream about something terrible; but will it be snakes, or will it be a railroad wreck, or will it be white horses trampling over you? Obviously, it may be a million different unpleasant things; and what is it that picks out this or that from the infinite store of your memory, and brings it into the region of half-consciousness which we call the dream?

Professor Freud's discovery is in brief that the dream is a wish-fulfillment. Our instincts present to our consciousness a great mass of impulses and desires, and among these the consciousness selects what it pleases, and represses and refuses to recognize or to act upon the others. But maybe these decisions are not altogether satisfactory to the subconsciousness. The mind of the body is in rebellion against the mind—shall we say of reason, or shall we say of society? The mind of society, otherwise known as the moral law, says that you shall be a good little boy, and shall go to school and learn what you are told, and on Sunday go to church and sit very still through a long sermon; whereas, the body of a boy would rather be a savage, hunting birds' nests and scalping enemies and exploring magic caves full of precious jewels. So the subconsciousness of the boy, balked and miserable, awaits its time, and finds its satisfaction when the boy is asleep and his moral censor has relaxed its control.

This dream mind is not a logical and orderly thing like the conscious mind; it is not business-like and civilized, it does not deal in abstractions. It is far more interested in things than in words; it does not present us with formulas, but with pictures, and with stories of weird and wonderful happenings. It is like the mind of the race, which we study in legends and religions. It does not tell us that the sun is a mass of incandescent hydrogen gas, so and so many miles in diameter; it tells us that the sun is a cosmic hero who slays the black dragon of night. So the mind of our body presents us with innumerable pictures and symbols, exactly such as we find in poetry. There may be, and frequently is, dispute as to just what a poet meant by this or that particular image, but if we read all the work of any particular poet, we get a certain impression of that poet's individuality. If he is always talking about the perfume of women's hair and the gleam of the white flesh of nymphs in the thickets, we are not left in doubt as to what is wrong with this poet.

And just so, when the expert sets to work to examine all the dreams that any one person can remember, day after day, sooner or later the expert observes that these dreams hover continually about one particular subject; and by questioning the person, he can find out what is the secret which is troubling the person, perhaps without the person himself being aware of it. Of course there are many people who like nothing so much as to talk about themselves; and many are spending their time and their money on the latest fad of being "psyched," who would, in any properly organized world, be put to work at hoeing weeds or washing their own clothes. Nevertheless, it is a fact that there are real mental disorders in the world, and innumerable honest and earnest people who have something the matter with them which they do not understand. Here is one way by which the conscientious investigator can find out what the trouble is, and make it clear to them, and by establishing harmony between their conscious and their subconscious minds, can many times put them in the way of health and happiness.

Through psychoanalysis we are enabled to understand the "split" personality and its cause. We discover that almost everyone has more or less rudimentary forms of multiple personality hidden within him; made out of desires and traits which he does not like, or which the world forces him to drive into the deeps of his being. These may be evil impulses, of sex or violence; they may be the most noble altruisms, or artistic yearnings, ridiculous things in a world of "hustle." A quite normal man or woman may keep a separate self, apart from the world, living a Jekyll life of business propriety and a Hyde life of religious or musical ecstasy. Or again, the repressed impulses may integrate themselves in the unconscious, and you may have genius or lunacy or both—"great wits to madness near allied." The modern knowledge on such dark mysteries you may find in Hart's "The Psychology of Insanity."

CHAPTER XIV

THE PROBLEM OF IMMORTALITY

(Discusses the survival of personality from the moral point of view: that is, have we any claim upon life, entitling us to live forever?)

As we explore the deeps of the subconsciousness, our own and other people's, we find ourselves confronting the strange question: Is it all our own mind, and that of other living people, or are we by any chance dealing with the minds of those who are dead? A great many earnest people, and some very learned people, are fully convinced that the latter is the case, and we have now to consider their arguments.

When I was a little boy I used to read and hear ghost stories, and would shudder over them; but I was given to understand that all this was just imagination, I must not take ghosts seriously, any more than fairies or dragons or nymphs or satyrs. For an educated person to take ghosts seriously—well, such a person would be almost as comical as that supremely comical person, the flying-machine man. Would you believe it, in those days there actually were people who believed they could learn to fly in the air, and spent their time manufacturing machines for this purpose! There was a scientist in Washington who had this "bug," and built himself a machine and started to fly, and fell into the Potomac river. We all laughed at him—we laughed so long and so loud that we killed the poor man; and then, a few years later, somebody took that machine of Professor Langley's and actually did fly with it! But that was after I had grown up a bit more, and was not quite so ready to laugh at an idea because it was new.

I remember vividly my first meeting with a man who believed in ghosts. He was a Unitarian clergyman, the Reverend Minot J. Savage of New York. I was sixteen years old, and just breaking out of my theological shell, and Doctor Savage helped to pry me loose. He was a grave and kindly man, of great learning and intelligence, and I remember vividly my consternation when one day he told me—oh, yes, he had seen many ghosts, he was accustomed to talk with ghosts every now and then. There was no doubt whatever that ghosts existed!

He told me many stories. I remember one so well that I do not have to go back to his books to look up the details. It was in the days before the Atlantic cable, and he had a friend who took a steamer to England. One night Doctor Savage was awakened and found the ghost of his friend standing by his bedside. The ship had gone down off the Irish coast, so the ghost declared, but the friend did not want Doctor Savage to think that he had suffered from the pangs of drowning; he had been struck on the left side of the head by a beam of the ship and had been killed instantly. Doctor Savage wrote down these circumstances and had them witnessed by a number of people, and two or three weeks later he received word that the body of his friend had been found on the Irish coast, with the left side of the head crushed in.

So then, of course, I studied the subject of ghosts. I have studied it off and on ever since, and have read most of the important new discoveries and arguments of the psychic researchers. To begin with, I will mention the contents of two large volumes, Gurney's "Phantasms of the Living." In this book are narrated many hundreds of cases, of which Doctor Savage's story is a type. It appears that persons at the moment of death, or in times of great mental stress, do somehow have the power to communicate with other people, even at the other side of the world. A few such cases might be attributed to coincidence or to fraud, but when you have so many cases, attested in minute detail by so many hundreds of otherwise honest people, you are not being scientific but simply stupid if you dismiss the whole subject with contempt.

Gurney discusses the phenomenon and its probable causes. We know, of course, that hallucinations are among the most common of psychic phenomenon. Your subconscious mind can be caused to see and hear and feel anything; likewise it has power to cause you to see and hear and feel anything. In practically all cases of multiple personality some of the split-off personalities can cause the others to see and hear and feel. And the consciousness, you must understand, takes these things to be just as real as real things; there is no way you can tell an hallucination from reality—except to ask other people about it. And if we admit the idea of telepathy, we may say that phantasms are hallucinations caused by this means; that is, the subconscious mind of your wife or your mother or your friend who is ill or dying, transmits to your subconscious mind some vivid impression, which causes your own subconscious mind to present to your consciousness a perfect image of that person, walking and talking with you, and your consciousness has no way of telling but that the image is real.

So much for phantasms of the living. But are there any phantasms of the dead? Are there any cases in which the time of the appearance can be proven to be subsequent to the time of death? Even this would not prove survival, of course; it is perfectly possible that the telepathic impulse might be delayed in our own minds, it might not flash into consciousness until our own state of mind made it possible. Can we say that there are cases in which the facts communicated are such as to convince us that the person was already dead, and was telling us something as a dead person and not as a living one?

Before we go into this question, let us clear the ground for the subject by discussing the survival of personality from a more general standpoint. What is it that we want to prove? What are the probabilities of its being true? What would be the consequences of its not being true? Have we any grounds, other than those of psychic research, for thinking that it is true, or that it may be true, or that it ought to be true? What, so to speak, are the morals of the doctrine of immortality?

Well, to begin with, the survival of the soul after death and forever is one of the principal doctrines of the Christian religion. Many devout Christians will read this book, and I will seem to them blasphemous when I say that this argument does not concern me. I count myself one of the lovers and friends of Jesus, I am presumptuous enough to believe that if he were on earth, I would understand him and get along with him excellently; but I do not know any reason why I should believe this, that, or the other doctrine about life because any religious sect, founded upon the name of Jesus, commands me so to believe. I see no more reason for adopting the idea of heaven because it is a Christian idea than I see for adopting the idea of reincarnation because it is a precious and holy idea to hundreds of millions of Buddhists. I have some very good friends who are Theosophists, and are quite convinced of this idea of reincarnation; that is, that the soul comes back into life over and over again in many different bodies, thus completing itself and renewing itself and expiating its sins. My Theosophist friends have a most elaborate and complicated body of what they consider to be knowledge on this subject; yet I have to take the liberty of saying that I cannot see that it has any relation to reality. It seems to me as completely unproven as any other fairy story, or myth, or legend—for example, the seven infernos of Dante, and the elaborate and complicated torments that are suffered there.

But, it will be argued, Jesus rose from the dead, and thus proved the immortality of the soul. Now, in the first place, there are many learned investigators who consider there is insufficient evidence for believing that Jesus ever lived; and certainly if this be so, it will be difficult to prove that he rose from the dead. Again, it was a common occurrence for crucified men not to die; sometimes it happened that their guards allowed them to be spirited away—even nowadays we have known of prison guards being bribed to allow a prisoner to escape. Again, the events of the return of Jesus may have been just such psychic phenomena as we are trying in this chapter to explain. Or, once more, they may have been purely legends. A very brief study will convince a thinking person that the people of that time were ready to believe anything, and to accept facts upon such authority, and to make them the basis for a scientific conclusion, is simply to be childish.

I shall be told, of course, that it is in the Bible, and therefore it must be true. The Bible is inspired, you say; and perhaps this is so. But then, a great deal of other literature is inspired, and that does not relieve me of the task of comparing these various inspirations, and judging them, and picking out what is of use to me. The Bible is the literature of the ancient Hebrews for a couple of thousand years. It represents what the race mind of a great people for one generation after another judged worth recording and preserving. You may get an idea what this means, if you will picture to yourself a large volume of English literature, containing some Teutonic myths, and the Saxon chronicles, and the "Morte d'Arthur," and several of Chaucer's stories, and some Irish fairy tales, and some of Bacon's essays, and Shakespeare's "Venus and Adonis," and the English prayer book, and the architect's specifications for Westminster Abbey, and a good part of "Burke's Peerage"; also Blackstone's "Commentaries," a number of Wesley's hymns, and Pope's "Essay on Man," and some chapters of Carlyle's "Past and Present," and Gladstone's speeches, and Blake's poems, and Captain Cook's story of his voyage around the world, and Southey's "Life of Nelson," and Morris's "News from Nowhere," and Blatchford's "Merrie England," and scores of pages from Hansard, which is the equivalent of our Congressional Record. You may find this description irreverent, but do not think it is meant so. Do me the honor to get out your Bible and look it over from this point of view!

But, you say, if we die altogether when we finish this earthly life, what becomes of moral responsibility and the punishment of sins? What shall we say to the wicked man to make him be good, if we cannot reward him with a heaven and frighten him with a hell? Well, my first answer is that we have been trying this process for a couple of thousand years, and the results seem to indicate that we might better seek out some other method of inducing men to behave themselves. They do not believe so completely in heaven and hell these days, but there were times in history when they did believe completely, and not merely were the believers just as cruel, they were just as treacherous and just as gluttonous and just as drunken. If you want to satisfy yourself on this point, I refer you to my book "The Profits of Religion," page 129.

Now, as a matter of fact, I think I can discern the outlines of a system of rewards and punishments automatically working in the life of men. I am not sure that I can prove that the wicked always get punished and the virtuous always rewarded; yet, when I stop and think, I am sure that I would not care to change places with any of the wicked people that I know in this world. Life may not always be "getting" them, but it has a way of "getting" their descendants, and I could not be entirely happy if I knew that my son and his sons were going to share the fate which I now observe befalling, for example, the grand dukes of Russia and their children. Life is one thing, and it does not exist for the individual, but for the race; its causes and effects do not always manifest themselves in one individual, but in a line of descendants. "Why are they called dynasties?" asked one of my professors of history; and a student brought the session to an end by answering: "Because that is what they always seem to do!"

But this is not perfect justice, you will argue. It is not perfect, from the point of view of you or me; but then, I ask, what else is there in the world that is perfect from that point of view? Why should our justice be any more perfect than, for example, our health or our thinking or our climate or our government? And, may it not very well be that our justice is up to us, in precisely the same way that some of these other things are up to us? Maybe what we have to do is to set to work to see to it that virtue does always get rewarded and vice does always get punished, right here and now, instead of waiting for an omnipotent God to attend to it in some hypothetical heaven.

I find this life of mine very wonderful, and enormously interesting. I am willing to take it on the terms that it is given, and to try to make the best of it; and I do not see that I have any right to dictate what shall be given me in some future life. If my father gives me a Christmas present, I am happy and grateful; and, of course, if I know that he is going to give me another present next Christmas, I am still more happy; but I do not see that I have any right to argue that because he gives me one Christmas present, he must give me an unlimited number of them, and I think it would be very ungrateful of me to refuse to thank him for a Christmas present until I had made sure that I was to get one next time!

Neither do I find myself such a wonderful person that I can assert that the morality of the universe absolutely depends upon the fact that I am immortal. Of course, I should like to live forever, and to know all the wonderful things that are going to happen in the world, and if it is true that I am so to live, I shall be immensely delighted. But I cannot say that it *must* be true, and all I can do is to investigate the probabilities. On this point my view is stated in a sentence of Spinoza's: "He who would love God rightly must not desire that God love him in return."

To sum up, the question of immortality is purely a question of fact. It is one to be approached in a spirit of open-minded inquiry, entirely unaffected by hopes or fears or dogmas or moral claims. It is worth while to get clear that we may be immortal, even though we do not now know it and cannot now prove it; it is possible that all psychic research might end in telepathy, and still, when we die, we might wake up and find ourselves alive. It might possibly be that some of us are immortal and not all of us. It might be that some parts of us are immortal and not the rest. It might be that our subconsciousness is immortal and not our consciousness. It might be that all of us, or some part of us, survive for a time, but not forever. This last is something which I myself am inclined to think may be the case.

Also, it seems worthwhile to mention that it is no argument against immortality that we cannot imagine it, that we cannot picture a universe consisting of uncountable billions of living souls, or what these souls would do to pass the time. It may very well be that among these souls there is no such thing as time. It may be that they are thoroughly occupied in ways beyond our imagining, or again, that they are not occupied, and under no necessity of being occupied. Let the person who presents such arguments begin by picturing to you how the brain cells manage to store up the uncounted millions of memories which you have, the thousands of words and combinations of words, and the thoughts which go with them, musical notes and tunes, colors and odors and visual impressions, memories of the past and hopes of the future and dreams that never were. Where are all those hundreds of millions of things, and what are they like when they are not in our consciousness, and how do they pass the time, and where were they in the hundreds of millions of years before we were born, and where will they be in the hundreds of millions of years of the future? When our wise men can answer these questions completely, it will be time enough for them to tell us about the impossibility of immortality.

CHAPTER XV

THE EVIDENCE FOR SURVIVAL

(Discusses the data of psychic research, and the proofs of spiritism thus put before us.)

Let us now take up the question of survival of personality after death from the strictly scientific point of view; let us consider what facts we have, and the indications they seem to give. First, we know that to all appearances the consciousness and the subconsciousness are bound up with the body. They grow with the body, they decline with the body, they seem to die with the body. We can irretrievably damage the consciousness by drawing a whiff of cyanogen gas into the lungs, or by sticking a pin into the brain, or by clogging one of its tiny blood vessels with waste matter. It is terrible to us to think that the mind of a great poet or prophet or statesman may be snuffed out of existence in such a way; but then, it is no argument against a fact to say that it is terrible. Insanity is terrible, war is terrible, pestilence is terrible, so also are tigers and poisonous snakes; but all these things exist, and all these things have power over the wisest and greatest mind, to put an end to its work on this earth at least.

And now we come with the new instrument of psychic research, to probe the question: What becomes of this consciousness when it disappears? Can we prove that it is still in existence, and is able by any method to communicate with us? Those who answer "Yes" argue that the mind of the dead person, unable to use its own bodily machinery any longer, manages in the hypnotic trance to use the bodily machinery of another person, called a "medium," and by it to make some kind of record to identify itself.

This, of course, is a strange idea, and requires a good deal of proof. The law of probability requires us not to accept an unlikely explanation, if there is any more simple one which can account for the facts. When we examine the product of automatic writing, table-tipping, and other psychic phenomena, we have first to ask ourselves, Is there anything in all this which cannot be explained by what we already know? Then, second, we have to ask, Is there any other supposition which will explain the facts, and which is easier to believe than the spirit theory?

These "spirits" apparently desire to convince us of their reality, and they tell us many things which are expected to convince us; they tell us things which we ourselves do not know, and which spirits might know. But here again we run up against the problem of the subconsciousness, with its infinite mass of "forgotten" knowledge. It is not so easy for the "spirits" to tell us things which we can be sure our subconscious mind could not possibly contain. Also, there comes the additional element of telepathy. It appears to be a fact that under trance conditions, or under any especially exciting conditions of the consciousness, one mind can reach out and take something out of another mind, or one mind can cause something to be passed over to another mind; and so information can be communicated to the mind of a medium, and can appear in automatic writing, or in clairvoyance, or in crystal gazing.

One of the most conscientious and earnest of all the investigators of this subject was the late Professor Hyslop, who many years ago sought to teach me "practical morality" (from the bourgeois point of view) in Columbia University. Professor Hyslop worked for fifteen years with a medium by the name of Mrs. Piper, who was apparently sincere and was never exposed in any kind of fraud. In Professor Hyslop's books you will find innumerable instances of amazing facts brought out in Mrs. Piper's trances. You will find Professor Hyslop arguing that the only way telepathy can account for these facts is by the supposition that there is a universal subconscious mind, or that the subconscious mind of the medium possesses the power to reach into the subconscious mind of every other living person and take out anything from it. But for my part, I cannot see that the case is quite so difficult. Professor Hyslop recites, for example, how Mrs. Piper would tell him facts about some long dead relative—facts which he did not know, but was later able to verify. But that proves simply nothing at all, because there could be no possible way for Professor Hyslop to be sure that he had never known these facts about his relatives. The facts might have been in his subconscious mind without having ever been in his conscious mind at all; he might have heard people talking about these matters while he was reading a book, or playing as a boy, paying no attention to what was said.

And then came Sir Oliver Lodge with his investigations. I will say this for his work—he was the first person who was able to make real to my mind the startling idea that perhaps after all the dead might be alive and able to communicate with us. You will find what he has to say in his book, "The Survival of Man," and it seems fair that a great scientist and a great man should have a chance to convince you of what seem to him the most important facts in the world.

Sir Oliver's son Raymond was killed in the war, and it is claimed that he began at once to communicate with his family. Among other things, he told them of the existence of a picture, which none of them had ever seen or heard of, a group photograph which he described in detail. But, of course, other people in this group knew of the existence of the photograph, and so we have again the possibility that some member of Sir Oliver's family may have taken into his subconscious mind without knowing it an impression or description of that picture. If you care to experiment, you will find that you can frequently play a part in the dreams of a child by talking to it in its sleep; and that is only one of a thousand different ways by which some member of a family might acquire, without knowing it, information of the existence of a photograph.

There is another possibility to be considered—that a portion of the consciousness may survive, and not necessarily forever. We are accustomed when death takes place to see the body before us, and we know that we can preserve the body for thousands of years if we wish. Why is it not possible that when conscious life is brought to a sudden end, there may remain some portion of the consciousness, or of the subconsciousness, cut off from the body, and slowly fading back into the universal mind energy, whatever we please to call it? There is a hard part of the body, the skeleton, which survives for some time; why might there not be a central core of the mind which is similarly tough and enduring? Of course, if consciousness is a function of the brain, it must decay as the brain decays; but how would it be if the brain were a function of the consciousness—which is, so far as I can see, quite as likely a guess.

I find many facts which seem to indicate the plausibility of this idea. I notice that in trance phenomena it is the spirits of those recently dead which seem to manifest the most vitality. Of course, you can go to any seance in the "white light" district of your city and receive communications from the souls of Cæsar and Napoleon and Alexander the Great and Pocahontas, and if the medium does not happen to be literary, you can communicate with Hamlet and Don Quixote and Siegfried and Achilles; but you will not find much reality about any of these people, they will not tell you very much about the everyday details of their lives. This fact that so much of what the "spirits" tell us is of our own time tends to cast doubt on the idea that the dead survive forever. How simple it would be to convince us, if the spirit of Sophocles would come back to earth and tell us where to dig in order to find copies of his lost tragedies! You would think that the soul of Sophocles, seeing our great need of beauty and wisdom, would be interested to give us his works! From genius, operating under the guidance of the conscious mind, we get sublimity, majesty and power; but what the trance mediums give us suggests, both in its moral and intellectual quality, the operation of the subconscious. It is exactly like what we get, for example, from dissociated personalities.

There are, to be sure, the books of Patience Worth, produced by the automatic writing of a lady in St. Louis, who tells us in evident good faith that her conscious personality is entirely innocent of Patience, and all her thought and doings. Patience writes long novels and dramas in a quaint kind of old English, and the lady in St. Louis knows nothing about this language. But does she positively know that when she was a child, she never happened to be in the room with someone who was reading old English aloud? Nothing seems more likely than that her subconscious mind heard some quaint, strange language, and took possession of it, and built up a personality around it, and even made a new language and a new literature from that starting point.

That is precisely the kind of thing in which the subconscious revels. It creates new characters, with an imagination infinite and inexhaustible. Who has not waked up and been astounded at the variety and reality of a dream? Who has not told his dreams and laughed over them? The subconscious will play at games, it will act and rehearse elaborate rôles; it will put on costumes, and delight in being Cæsar and Napoleon and Alexander the Great and Pocahontas and Hamlet and Don Quixote and Siegfried and Achilles. Yes, it will even play at being "spirits"! It will be mischievous and impish; it will be swallowed up with a sense of its own importance, taking an insolent delight in convincing the world's most learned scientists of the fact that its play-acting is reality. It will call itself "Raymond" to move and thrill a grief-stricken family; it will call itself "Phinuit" and "Dr. Hodgson," and cause an earnest professor of "practical morality" to give up a respectable position in Columbia University and write books to convince the world that the dead are sending him messages.

Consider, for example, the multiple personality of Miss Beauchamp. Remember that here we are not dealing with any guess work about "spirits"; here we have half a dozen different "controls," none of them the least bit dead, but all of them a part of the consciousness of one entirely alive young lady. A specialist has spent some six years investigating the case, day after day, week after week, writing down the minute details of what happens. And now consider the miscreant known as "Sally." Sally is just as real as any child whom you ever held in your arms. Sally has love and hate, fear and hope, pain and delight—and Sally is a little demon, created entirely out of the subconsciousness of a highly refined and conscientious young college graduate of Boston. Sally spends Miss Beauchamp's money on candy, and eats it; Sally pawns Miss Beauchamp's watch and deliberately loses the ticket; Sally uses Miss Beauchamp's lips and tongue to tell lies about Miss Beauchamp; Sally strikes Miss Beauchamp dumb, or makes her hear exactly the opposite of what is spoken to her. Yes, and Sally pleads and fights frantically for her life; Sally enters into intrigues with other parts of Miss Beauchamp, and for years deliberately fools Doctor Prince, who is her Recording Angel and Heavenly Judge!

And can anybody doubt that Sally could have fooled a grieving mother, and made that mother think she was talking to the ghost of a long lost child? Can anybody doubt that Sally could and would play the part of any person she had ever known, or of any historic character she had ever read about? And don't overlook the all-important fact that the conscious Miss Beauchamp was absolutely innocent of all this, and was horrified when she was told about it. So here you have the following situation, no matter of guesswork, but definitely established: your dearest friend may act as a medium, and in all good faith may bring to the surface some part of his or her subconsciousness, which masquerades before you in a hundred different rôles, and plays upon you with deliberate malice the most subtle and elaborate and cruel tricks.

And how much worse the situation becomes when to this there is added the possibility of conscious fraud! When the medium is a person who is taking your money, and thrives by making you believe in the "spirits" she produces! You may go to Lily Dale, in New York state, the home of the Spiritualists, where they have a convention every summer, and in row after row of tents you may hear, and even see, every kind of spirit you ever dreamed of, ringing bells and shaking tambourines and dancing jigs. And you may see poor farmers' wives, with tears streaming down their cheeks, listening to the endearments of their dead children, and to wisdom from the lips of Oliver Wendell Holmes speaking with a Bowery accent. This kind of thing was exposed many years ago by Will Irwin in a book called "The Medium Game"; and then—after traveling from one kind of medium to another, and studying all their frauds, Irwin tells how he went into a "parlor" on Sixth Avenue, and there by a fat old woman who had never seen him before, was suddenly told the most intimate secrets of his life!

It has recently been announced that Thomas A. Edison is at work upon a device to enable spirits to communicate with the living, if there really are spirits seeking to do this. It is Edison's idea that spirits may inhabit some kind of infinitely rarefied astral body, and he proposes to manufacture an instrument which is sensitive to an impression many millions of times fainter than anything the human body can feel. This should make it easier for the spirits, and should constitute a fairer test, possibly a decisive one. When that machine is perfected and put to work by scientific men, I wish to suggest a few tests which will convince me that there really are spirits, and that the results are not to be explained by telepathy.

First, assuming that the spirits live forever, there are some useful things which were known to the people of ancient time, and are not known to anyone living now. For example, let one of the Egyptian craftsmen come forward and tell us the secret of their glass-staining, which I understand is now a lost art. And then Sophocles, as I have already suggested, will tell us where we can find his lost dramas; or if he doesn't know where any copies are buried, let him find in the spirit world some scribe or librarian or book-lover who can give us this priceless information. All over the ancient lands are buried and forgotten cities, and in those cities are papyrus scrolls and graven tablets and bricks. Infinite stores of knowledge are thus concealed from us; and how simple for the ancient ones who possess this information to make it known to us, and so to convince us of their reality!

Or, again, supposing that spirits are not immortal, but that they slowly fade from life as do their bodies. Suppose that a Raymond Lodge or other recently dead soldier wishes to communicate with his father and to convince his father that it is really an independent being, and not simply a part of the father's subconscious mind—let him try something like this. Let the father write six brief notes, and put them in six envelopes all alike, and shuffle them up and put them in a hat and draw out one of them. Now, assuming that the experimenter is honest, there is no living human being who knows the contents of that envelope, and if the medium is dipping into the subconscious mind of the experimenter, the chances are one in six of the right note being hit upon. Assuming that spirits may not be able to get inside an envelope and read a folded letter, there is no objection to the experimenter, provided he is honest, and provided there are no mirrors or other tricks, holding the envelope behind his back, and tearing it open, and spreading it out for the convenience of the spirit. And now, if the spirit can read that letter correctly every time, we shall be fairly certain that whatever force we are dealing with, it is not the subconscious mind of the experimenter.

Or, let us take another test. Let us have a roulette wheel in a covered box, or hidden away so that no one but the spirit can see it. We spin the wheel, and any one of the habitues of Monte Carlo can figure out the chance of the little ball dropping into any particular number. If now the spirit can tell us each time where we shall find the ball, we shall know that we are dealing with knowledge which does not exist either in the conscious or the subconscious mind of any living human being.

Among the things that "spirits" have been accustomed to do, since the days when they first made their appearance with the Fox sisters in America, are the lifting of tables and the ringing of bells and the assuming of visible forms. These are what is known as "materializations," and when I was a boy, and used to hear people talking about these things, there was always one test required: let the materializations manifest themselves upon recording instruments scientifically devised; let photographs be taken of them, let them be weighed and measured, and so on. Well, time has moved forward, and these tests have been met, and it appears that "materializations" are facts—although it is still as uncertain as ever what they are materializations of. An English scientist, Professor Crawford, has published a book entitled "The Reality of Psychic Phenomena," in which he tells the results of many years of testing materializations by the strictest scientific methods. When the medium "levitates" a table—that is, causes it to go up in the air without physical contact—it appears that her own weight increases by exactly the weight of the table. When she exerts any force, which apparently she can do at a distance, the recording instruments show the exact counter-force in her own body.

The results of these investigations are calculated at first to take your breath away. It begins to appear that the theosophists may be right, and that we may have one or more "astral" bodies within or coincident with the physical body; and that under the trance conditions we mold and make over this "astral" body in accordance with our imaginations, precisely as a sculptor molds the clay. At any rate, our subconsciousness has the power to project from it masses of substance, and to cause these to take all kinds of forms, for example, human faces, which have been photographed innumerable times. Or the body can shoot out long rods or snaky projections, which lift tables, and exert force which has been recorded upon pressure instruments and weighed by scales.

As I write, a friend lends me a fifteen-dollar volume, a translation just published of an elaborate work by Baron von Schrenck-Notzing, a physician of Munich, giving minute details of four years' experiments in this field. So rigid was this investigator in his efforts to exclude fraud, that not merely was the medium stripped and sewed up in black tights, but the "cabinet" in which she sat was a big sack of black cloth, everywhere sewed tight by machine. Every crevice of the medium's body was searched before and after the tests, and every inch of the "cabinet" gone over. The investigators sat within a couple of feet of the medium, and would draw back the curtains, and while holding her hands and her feet, would watch great masses of filmy gray and white stuff exude from the medium's mouth, from her armpits and breasts and sides. This would happen in red light of a hundred candle power, by which print could be easily read; and the medium would herself illuminate the phenomena with a red electric torch. The investigators would be privileged to examine these "phantom" forms, to touch them gently, and be touched by them—soft and slimy, like the tongue of an animal; but sometimes the things would misbehave, and strike them in the eye, hurting them.

The medium, a young French girl living in the home of the wife of a well-known French playwright, had begun with spiritualist ideas, but came to take a matter-of-fact attitude to what happened, and in her trances would labor to mold these emanations into hands or faces, as requested by those present. She finally succeeded in allowing them to separate the soft mucous stuff from her body, and keep it for chemical and bacteriological examination. All this time she would be surrounded by a battery of cameras, nine at once, some of them inside the cabinet; and when the desired emanation was in sight, all these cameras would be set off by flashlight, and in the book you have over two hundred such photographs, showing faces and hands from every point of view. There are even moving-pictures, showing the material coming out of her mouth and going back!

It is evident that we have here a whole universe of unexplored phenomena; and it seems that many of the old-time superstitions which were dumped overboard have now to be dragged back into the boat and examined in the light of new knowledge. What could smack more of magic and fraud than crystal-gazing? Yet it appears that the subconsciousness has power to project an image of its hidden memories into a crystal ball, where it may be plainly seen. We find so well-recognized an authority as Dr. Morton Prince using this method to enable one of the many Miss Beauchamps to recall incidents in her previous life which were otherwise entirely lost to her. Likewise this exploration of the disintegration of personality enables us to watch in the making all the phenomena of trance and ecstasy which have had so much to do with the making of religions. We know now how Joan of Arc heard the "voices," and we can make her hear more voices or make her stop hearing voices, as we prefer. Also we know all about demons and "demoniac possession." We can cast out demons—and without having to cause them to enter a herd of swine! We may some day be prepared to investigate the wonder stories which the Yogis tell us, about their ability to leave their physical bodies in a trance, and to appear in England at a few moments' notice for the transaction of their spiritual business!

But we want things proven to us, and we don't want the people with whom we work to be animated either by religious fanaticism or by money greed. We are ready to unlimber our minds, and prepare for long journeys into strange regions, but we want to move cautiously, and choose our route carefully, and be sure we do not lose our way! We want to deal rationally with life; we don't want to make wild guesses, or to choose a complicated and unlikely solution when a simple one will suffice. But, on the other hand, we must be alive to the danger of settling down on our little pile of knowledge, and refusing to take the trouble to investigate any more. That is a habit of learned men, I am sorry to say; the law of inertia applies to the scientist, as well as to the objects he studies. The scientists of our time have had to be prodded into considering each new discovery about the subconscious mind, precisely as the scientists of Galileo's time had to be prodded to watch him drop weights from the tower of Pisa. When he told them that the earth moved round the sun instead of the sun round the earth, they tortured him in a dungeon to make him take it back, and he did so, but whispered to himself, "And yet it moves." And it did move, of course, and continued to move. And in exactly the same way, if it be true that we have these hidden forces in us, they will continue to manifest themselves, and masses of people will continue to flock to Lily Dale, and to pay out their hard-earned money, until such a time as our learned men set to work to find out the facts and tell us how we can utilize these forces without the aid of either superstition or charlatanry.

CHAPTER XVI

THE POWERS OF THE MIND

(Sets forth the fact that knowledge is freedom and ignorance is slavery, and what science means to the people.)

We have now completed a brief survey of the mind and its powers. Whatever we may have proved or failed to prove, this much we may say with assurance: the reader who has followed our brief sketch attentively has been disabused of any idea he may have held that he knows it all; and this is always the first step towards knowledge.

The mind is the instrument whereby our race has lifted itself out of beasthood. It is the instrument whereby we hold ourselves above the forces which seek to drag us down, and whereby we shall lift ourselves higher, if higher we are to go. How shall we protect this precious instrument? How shall we complete our mastery of it? What are the laws of the conduct of the mind?

The process of the mind is one of groping outward after new facts, and digesting and assimilating them, as the body gropes after and digests and assimilates food. The senses bring us new impressions, and we take these and analyze them, tear them into the parts which compose them, compare them with previous sensations, recognize difference in things which seem to be alike, and resemblances in things which seem to be different; we classify them, and provide them with names, which are, as it were, handles for the mind to grasp. Above all, we seek for causes; those chains of events which make what we know as order in the world of phenomena. And when the mind has what seems to be a cause, it proceeds to test it according to methods it has worked out, the rules and principles of experimental science.

It is a comparatively small number of sensations which the body brings to the mind of itself; it is a narrow world in which we should live if our minds adopted a passive attitude toward life. But some minds possess what we call curiosity; they set out upon their own impulse to explore life; they discover new laws and make new experiences and new sensations for themselves. The mind forms an idea, and at first, after the fashion of the ancient Greek philosophers, it glorifies that idea and sets it in the seat of divinity. But presently comes the empirical method, which refuses authority to any idea unless it can stand the test of experiment, and prove that it corresponds with reality. Nowadays the thinker amasses his facts, and forms a theory to explain them, and then proceeds to try out this theory by the most rigid method that he or his critics can devise. If the theory doesn't "work"—that is, if it doesn't explain all the facts and stand all the tests—it is thrown away like a worn-out shoe. So little by little a body of knowledge is built up which is real knowledge; which will serve us in our daily lives, which we can use as foundation-stones in the structure of our civilization.

By this method of research man is expanding his universe beyond anything that could have been conceived in the pre-scientific days. Hour by hour, while we work and play and sleep, the mind of our race is discovering new worlds in which our posterity will dwell. For uncounted ages man walked upon the earth, surrounded by infinite swarms of bacterial life of whose existence he never dreamed. The invisible rays of the spectrum beat upon him, and he knew nothing of what they did to him, whether good or evil. He lifted his head and saw vast universes of suns, in comparison with which his world was a mere speck of dust; yet to him these universes were globes or lanterns which some divinity had hung in the sky.

One of the most fascinating illustrations of how the mind runs ahead of the senses is the story of the planet Uranus, which, less than two hundred years ago, had never been beheld by the eye of man. A mathematician seated in his study, working over the observations of other planets, their motions in relation to their mass and distance, discovered that their behavior was not as it should be. At certain times none of them were in quite the right place, and he decided that this variation must be due to the existence of an unknown body. He worked out the problem of what must be the mass and the exact orbit of this body, in order for it to be responsible for the variations observed; and when he had completed these calculations, he announced to the astronomical world, "Turn your telescopes to a certain spot in the heavens at a certain minute of a certain night, and you will find a new planet of a certain size." And so for the first time the human senses became aware of a fact, which by themselves they might not have discovered in all eternity.

Now, the importance of exact knowledge concerning a new planet may not be apparent to the ordinary man; but if the thing which is discovered is, for example, an unknown ray which will move an engine or destroy a cancer, then we realize the worthwhileness of research, and the masters of the world's commerce are willing to give here and there a pittance for the increase of such knowledge. But men of science, who have by this time come to a sense of their own dignity and importance, understand that there is no knowledge about reality which is useless, no research into nature which is wasted. You might say that to describe and classify the fleas which inhabit the bodies of rats and ground-squirrels, and to study under the microscope the bacteria which live in the blood of these fleas—that this would be an occupation hardly worthy of the divinity that is in man. But presently, as a result of this knowledge about fleas and flea diseases being in existence and available, a bacteriologist discovers the secret of the dread bubonic plague, which hundreds of times in past history has wiped out a great part of the population of Europe and Asia.

Mark Twain tells in his "Connecticut Yankee" how his hero was able to overcome the wizard Merlin, because he knew in advance of an eclipse of the sun. And this was fiction, of course; but if you prefer fact, you may read in the memoirs of Houdin, the French conjurer, how he was able to bring the Arab tribes into subjection to the French government by depriving the great chieftains of their strength. He gathered them into a theatre, and invited their mighty men upon the stage, and there was an iron weight, and they were able to lift it when Houdin permitted, and not to lift it when he forbade. These noble barbarians had never heard of the electro-magnet, and could not conceive of a force that could operate through a solid wooden floor beneath their feet.

Such things, trivial as they are, serve to illustrate the difference between ignorance and knowledge, and the power which knowledge gives. The man who knows is godlike to those who do not know; he may enslave them, he may do what he pleases with their lives, and they are powerless to help themselves. Anyone who would help them must begin by giving them knowledge, real knowledge. There is no such thing as freedom without knowledge, and it must be the best knowledge, it must be new knowledge; he who goes against new knowledge armed with old knowledge is like the Chinese who went out to meet machine-guns with bows and arrows, and with umbrellas over their heads.

Once upon a time knowledge was the prerogative of kings and priests and ruling castes; but this supreme power has been wrested from them, and this is the greatest step in human progress so far taken. "Seek and ye shall find," is the law concerning knowledge today. "Knock, and it shall be opened unto you." In this, my Book of the Mind, I say to you that knowledge is your priceless birthright, and that you should repudiate all men and all institutions and all creeds and all formulas which seek to keep this heritage from you. Beware of men who bid you believe something because it is told you, or because your fathers believed it, or because it is written in some ancient book, or embodied in some ancient ceremonial. Break the chains of these venerable spells; and at the same time beware of the modern spells which have been contrived to replace them! Beware of party cries and shibboleths, the idols of the forum, as Plato called them, the prejudices which are set as snares for your feet. Beware of cant—that paraphernalia of noble sentiments, artificially manufactured by politicians and newspapers for the purpose of blinding you to their knaveries. Remember that you live in a world of class conflicts; at every moment of your life your mind is besieged by secret enemies, it is exposed to poison gas-clouds deliberately released by people who seek to make use of you for purposes which are theirs and not yours. In the fairy-tales we used to love, the hero was provided with magic protection against the perils of those times; but what hero and what magic will guard the modern man against the propaganda of militarism, nationalism, and capitalist imperialism?

The mind is like the body in that it can be trained, it can be taught sound habits, its powers can be enormously increased. There are many books on mind and memory training, some of which are useful, and some of which are trash. There is an English system widely advertised, called "Pelmanism," of which I have personally made no test, but it has won endorsements of a great many people who do not give their endorsements lightly.

This is the subject of applied psychology, and just as in medicine, or in law, or in any of the arts, there is a vast amount of charlatanry, but there is also genuine knowledge being patiently accumulated and standardized. When the United States government had to have an army in a hurry it did not make its millions of young men into teamsters or aviators at random. It used the new methods of determining reaction times, and testing the coordination of mind and body. Recently I visited the Whittier Reform School in California, where delinquent boys are educated by the state. A boy had been set to work in the tailor shop, and it had been found that he was unable to make the buttons and the buttonholes of a coat come in the right place. For nine years the state of California, and before it the state of Georgia, had been laboring to teach this boy to make buttons and buttonholes meet; the effort had cost some five thousand dollars, to say nothing of all the coats which were spoiled, and all the mental suffering of the victim and his teachers. Finally someone persuaded the state of California to spend a few thousand dollars and install a psychological bureau for the purpose of testing all the inmates of the institution; so by a half hour's examination the fact was developed that this boy was mentally defective. Although he was eighteen years old in body, his mind was only eight years old, and so he would never be able to achieve the feat of making buttons and buttonholes meet.

This is a new science which you may read about in Terman's "The Measurement of Intelligence." By testing normal children, it is established that certain tasks can be performed at certain ages. A child of three can point to his eyes, his nose and his mouth; he can repeat a sentence of six syllables, and repeat two digits, and give his family name. Older children are asked to look at a picture and then tell what they saw; to note omissions in a picture, to arrange blocks according to their weight, to arrange words into sentences, to note absurdities in statements, to count backwards, and to make change. Children of fifteen are asked to interpret fables, to reverse the hands of a clock, and so on. Of course there are always variations; every child will be better at some kinds of tests than at others. But by having a wide variety, and taking the average, you establish a "mental age" for the child—which may be widely different from its physical age. You may find some whose minds have stopped growing altogether, and can only be made to grow by special methods of education. Enlightened communities are now conducting separate schools for defective children—replacing the old-fashioned schoolmaster who wore out birch-rods trying to force poor little wretches to learn what was beyond their power.

In the same way psychology can be applied in industry, and in the detection of crime. Here, too, there is a vast amount of "fake," but also the beginning of a science. Our laws do not as yet permit the use of automatic writing and the hypnotic trance in the investigation of crime, but they have sometimes permitted some of the simpler tests, for example, those of memory association. The examiner prepares a list of a hundred names of objects, and reads those names one after another, and asks the person he is investigating to name the first thing which is suggested to him by each word in turn. "Engine" will suggest "steam," or perhaps it will suggest "train"; "coat" will suggest "trousers," or perhaps it will suggest "pocket," and so on. The examiner holds a stop-watch, and notes what fraction of a second each one of these reactions takes. The ordinary man, who is not trying to conceal anything, will give all his associations promptly, and the reaction times will be approximately alike. But suppose the man has just murdered somebody with an axe, and buried the body in a cellar with a fire shovel, and taken a pocketbook, and a watch, and a locket, and a number of various objects, and climbed out of the cellar window by breaking the glass; and now suppose that in his list of a hundred objects the psychologist introduces unexpectedly a number of these things. In each case the first memory association of the criminal will be one which he does not wish to give. He will have to find another, and that inevitably takes time. One or two such delays might be accidental; but if every time there is any suggestion of the murder, or the method or scene of the murder, there is noticed confusion and delay, you may be sure that the conscious mind is interfering with the subconscious mind. The difference between the conscious and the subconscious mind is always possible to detect, and if you are permitted to be thorough in your experiments, you can make certain what is in the subconscious mind that the conscious mind is trying to conceal.

Here, as everywhere in life, knowledge is power, and expert knowledge confers mastery over the shrewdest untrained mind. The only trouble is that under our present social system the trained mind is very apt to be working in the interest of class privilege. The psychologist who is employed by a great corporation, or by a police department, may be as little worthy of trust as a chemist who is engaged in making poison gases to be used by capitalist imperialism for the extermination of its rebellious slaves. But what this proves is not that scientific knowledge is untrustworthy, but merely that the workers must acquire it, they must have their own organizations and their own experiments in every field. To give knowledge to the masses of mankind, slow and painful as the process seems, is now the most important task confronting the enlightened thinker.

The method of psychoanalysis gives us also much insight into the phenomena of genius, and the hope that we may ultimately come to understand it. At present we are embarrassed because genius is so often closely allied to eccentricity; the supernormal appears in connection with the subnormal—and it is often hard to tell them apart. Great poets and painters in revolt against a world of smug commercialism, adopt irresponsibility as their religion; they live in a world of their own, they dress like freaks, they refuse to pay their debts, or to be true to their wives. They are followed by a host of disciples, who adopt the defects of the master as a substitute for his qualities. And so there grows up a perverted notion of what genius is, and wholly false standards of artistic quality. There is nothing mankind needs more than sure and exact tests of mental superiority; not merely the ability to acquire languages and to solve mathematical equations, but the ability to carry in the mind intense emotions, while at the same time shaping and organizing them by the logical faculty, selecting masses of facts and weaving them into a pattern calculated to awaken the emotion in others. This is the last and greatest work of the human spirit, and to select the men who can do it, and foster their activity, is the ultimate purpose of all true science.

CHAPTER XVII

THE CONDUCT OF THE MIND

(Concludes the Book of the Mind with a study of how to preserve and develop its powers for the protection of our lives and the lives of all men.)

Someone wrote me the other day, asking, "When is the best time to acquire knowledge?" I answer, "The time is now." It is easier to learn things when you are young, but you cannot be young when you want to be, and if you are old, the best time to acquire knowledge is when you are old. It is true that the brain-cells seem to harden like the body, and it is less easy for them to take on new impressions; but it can be done, and just as Seneca began to learn Greek at eighty, I know several old men whom the recent war has shaken out of their grooves of thought and compelled to deal with modern ideas.

But if you are young, then so much the better! Then the divine thrill of curiosity is keenest; then your memory is fresh, and can be trained; your mind is plastic, and you can form sound habits. You can teach yourself to respect truth and to seek it, you can teach yourself accuracy, open-mindedness, flexibility, persistence in the search for understanding.

First of all, I think, is accuracy. Learn to think straight! Let your mind be as a sharp scalpel, penetrating unrealities and falsehoods, cutting its way to the facts. When you set out to deal with a certain subject, acquire mastery of it, so that you can say, "I know." And yet, never be too sure that you know! Never be so sure, that you are not willing to consider new facts, and to change your way of thinking if it should be necessary. I look about me at the world, and see tigers and serpents, dynamite and poison gas and forty-two centimeter shells—yet I see nothing in the world so deadly to men as an error of the mind. Look at the mental follies about you! Look at the prejudices, the delusions, the lies deliberately maintained—and realize the waste of it all, the pity of it all!

Every man, it seems, has his pet delusions, which he hugs to his bosom and loves because they are his own. If you try to deprive him of those delusions, it is as though you tore from a woman's arms the child she has borne. I have written a book called "The Profits of Religion," and never a week passes that there do not come to me letters from people who tell me they have read this book with pleasure and profit, they are grateful to me for teaching them so much about the follies and delusions of mankind, and it is all right and all true, save for two or three pages, in which I deal with the special hobby which happens to be their hobby! What I say about all the other creeds is correct—but I fail to understand that the Mormon religion is a dignified and inspired religion, a gift from on high, and if only I would carefully study the "Book of Mormon," I would realize my error! Or it is all right, except what I say about the Christian Scientists, or the Theosophists, or perhaps one particular sect of the Theosophists, who are different from the others. Today there lies upon my desk a letter from a man who has read many of my books, and now is grief-stricken because he must part company from me; he discovers that I permit myself to speak disrespectfully about the Seventh Day Adventist religion, whereas he is prepared to show the marvels of biblical prophecy now achieving themselves in the world. How could any save a divinely revealed religion have foreseen the present movement to establish the Sabbath by law? Yes, and presently I shall see the last atom of the prophecy fulfilled—there will be a death penalty for failure to obey the Sabbath law!

Cultivate the great and precious virtue of open-mindedness. Keep your thinking free, not merely from outer compulsions, but from the more deadly compulsions of its own making—from prejudices and superstitions. The prejudices and superstitions of mankind are like those diseased mental states which are discovered by the psychoanalyst; what he calls a "complex" in the subconscious mind, a tangle or knot which is a center of disturbance, and keeps the whole being in a state of confusion. Each group of men, each sect or class, have their precious dogmas, their shibboleths, their sacred words and stock phrases which set their whole beings aflame with fanaticism. They have also their phobias, their words of terror, which cannot be spoken in their presence without causing a brain-storm.

At present the dread word of our time is "Communist."

You can scarcely say the word without someone telephoning for the police. And yet, when you meet a Communist, what is he? A worn and fragile student, who has thought out a way to make the world a better place to live in, and whose crime is that he tells others about his idea! Or perhaps you belong to the other side, and then your word of terror is the word

"Capitalist." You meet a Capitalist, and what do you find? Very likely you find a man who is kindly, generous in his personal impulses, but bewildered, possibly a little frightened, still more irritated and made stubborn. So you realize that nearly all men are better than the institutions and systems under which they live; you realize the urgent need of applying your reasoning powers to the problem of social reorganization.

Cultivate also, in the affairs of your mind, the ancient virtue of humility. There is an oldtime poem, which perhaps was in your school readers, "Oh, why should the spirit of mortal be proud?" My answer is, for innumerable reasons. The spirit of mortal should be proud and must be proud because life throbs in it, and because life is a marvelous thing, and the excitement of life is perpetual. Yesterday I met a young mother; and of what avail is all the pessimism of poets against the pride of a young mother? "Oh!" she cried, and her face lighted up with delight. "He said 'Goo'!" Yes, he said "Goo!"—and never since the world began had there been a baby which had achieved that marvel. Presently it will be, "Look, look, he is trying to walk!" Then he will be getting marks at school, and presently he will be displaying signs of genius. Always it will take an effort of the mind of that young mother to realize that there are other children in the world as wonderful as her own; and perhaps it will take many generations of mental effort before there will be young mothers capable of realizing that some other child is more wonderful than her child.

In other words, it is by a definite process of broadening our minds that we come to realize the lives of others, to transfer to them the interest we naturally take in our own lives, and to admit them to a state of equality with ourselves. This is one of the services the mind must render for us; it is the process of civilizing us. And there is another, and yet more important task, which is to make clear to us the fact that we do not altogether make this life of ours, that there is a universe of power and wisdom which is not ours, but on which we draw. "The fear of the Lord is the beginning of wisdom," said the Psalmist. We know now that fear is an ugly emotion, destructive to life; but it may be purified and made into a true humility, which every thinking man must feel towards life and its miracles.

Also the man will have joy, because it is given him to share the high, marvelous adventure of being. To the pleasures of the body there is a limit, and it comes quickly; but the pleasures of the mind are infinite, and no one who truly understands them can have a moment of boredom in life. To a man who possesses the key to modern thought, who knows what knowledge is and where to look for it, the life of the mind is a panorama of delight perpetually unrolled before him. To the minds of our ancestors there was one universe; but to our minds there are many universes, and new ones continually discovered.

The only question is, which one will you choose? Will you choose the universe of outer space, the material world of infinity? Consider the smallest insect that you can see, crawling upon the surface of the earth; small as that insect is in relation to the earth, it is not so small, by millions of times, as is the earth in relation to the universe made visible to our eyes by the high-power telescope, plus the photographic camera, plus the microscope. If you want to know the miracles of this world of space, read Arrhenius' "The Life of the Universe," or Simon Newcomb's "Sidelights on Astronomy." Suffice it here to say that we have a chemistry of the stars, by means of the spectroscope; that we can measure the speed and direction of stars by the same means; that we have learned to measure the size of the stars, and are studying stars which we cannot even see! And then along comes Einstein, with his theories of "relativity," and makes it seem that we have to revise a great part of this knowledge to allow for the fact that not merely everything we look at, but also we ourselves, are flying every which way through space!

Or will you choose the universe of the atom, the infinity of the material world followed the other way, so to speak? Big as is the universe in relation to our world, and big as is our world in relation to the insect that crawls on it, the insect is bigger yet in relation to the molecules which compose its body; and these in turn are millions of millions of times bigger than the atoms which compose them; and then, behold, in the atom there are millions of millions of electrons—tiny particles of electric energy! We cannot see these infinitely minute things, any more than we can see the electricity which runs our trolley cars; but we can see their effects, and we can count and measure them, and deal with them in complicated mathematical formulas, and be just as certain of their existence as we are of the dust under our feet. If you wish to explore this wonderland, read Duncan's "The New Knowledge," or Dr. Henry Smith Williams' "Miracles of Science."

Or will you choose the universe of the subconscious, our racial past locked up in the secret chambers of our mind? Or will you choose the universe of the superconscious, the infinity of genius manifested in the arts? By the device of art man not merely creates new life, he tests it, he weighs it and measures it, he tries experiments with it, as the physicist with the molecule and the astronomer with light. He finds out what works, and what does not work, and so develops his moral and spiritual muscles, training himself for his task as maker of life.

Written words can give but a feeble idea of the wonders that are found in these enchanted regions of the mind. Here are palaces of splendor beyond imagining, here are temples with sacred shrines, and treasure-chambers full of gold and priceless jewels. Into these places we enter as Aladdin in the ancient tale; we are the masters here, and all that we see is ours. He who has once got access to it—he possesses not merely the magic lamp, he possesses all the wonderful fairy properties of all the tales of our childhood. His is the Tarnhelm and the magic ring which gives him power over his foes; his is the sword Excalibur which none can break, and the silver bullet which brings down all game, and the flying carpet upon which to travel over the earth, and the house made of ginger-bread, and the three wishes which always come true, and the philter of love, and the elixir of youth, and the music of the spheres, and—who knows, some day he may come upon heaven, with St. Peter and his golden key, and the seraphim singing, and the happy blest conversing!

CHAPTER XVIII

THE UNITY OF THE BODY

(Discusses the body as a whole, and shows that health is not a matter of many different organs and functions, but is one problem of one organism.)

The reader who has followed our argument this far will understand that we are seldom willing to think of the body as separate from the mind. The body is a machine, to be sure, but it is a machine that has a driver, and while it is possible for a sound machine to have a drunken and irresponsible driver, such a machine is not apt to remain sound very long. Frequently, when there is trouble with the machine, we find the fault to be with the driver; in other words, we find that what is needed for the body is a change in the mind.

If you wish to have a sound body, and to keep it sound as long as possible, the first problem for you to settle is what you want to make of your life; you must have a purpose, and confront the tasks of life with energy and interest. What is the use of talking about health to a man who has no moral purpose? He may answer—indeed, I have heard victims of alcoholism answer—"Let me alone. I have a right to go to hell in my own way."

I am aware, of course, that the opposite of the proposition is equally true. A man cannot enjoy much mental health while he has a sick body. It is a good deal like the old question, Which comes first, the hen or the egg? The mind and the body are bound up together, and you may try to deal with each by turn, but always you find yourself having to deal with both. Most physicians have a tendency to overlook the mind, and Christian Scientists make a religion of overlooking the body, and each pays the penalty in greatly reduced effectiveness.

My first criticism of medical science, as it exists today, is that it has a tendency to concentrate upon organs and functions, and to overlook the central unity of the system. You will find a doctor who specializes in the stomach and its diseases, and is apt to talk as if the stomach were a thing that went around in the world all by itself. He will discuss the question of what goes into your stomach, and overlook to point out to you that your stomach is nourished by your blood-stream, which is controlled by your nervous system, which in turn is controlled by hope, by ambition, by love, by all the spiritual elements of your being. A single pulse of anger or of fear may make more trouble with the contents of your stomach than the doctor's pepsins and digestive ferments can remedy in a week.

Of course, you may do yourself some purely local injury, and so for a time have a purely local problem. You may smash your finger, and that is a problem of a finger; but neglect it for a few days, and let blood poison set in, and you will be made aware that the human body is one organism, and also that, in spite of any metaphysical theories you may hold, your body does sometimes dominate and control your mind.

Some one has said that the blood is the life; and certainly the blood is both the symbol and the instrument of the body's unity. The blood penetrates to all parts of the body and maintains and renews them. If the blood is normal, the work of renewal does not often fail. If there is a failure of renewal—that is, a disease—we shall generally find an abnormal condition of the blood. The distribution of the blood is controlled by the heart, a great four-chambered pump. One chamber drives the blood to the lungs, a mass of fine porous membranes, where it comes into contact with the air, and gives off the poisons which it has accumulated in its course through the body, and takes up a fresh supply of oxygen. By another chamber of the heart the blood is then sucked out of the lungs, and by the next chamber it is driven to every corner of the body. It takes to every cell of the body the protein materials which are necessary for the body's renewal, and also the fuel materials which are to be burned to supply the body's energy; also it takes some thirty million millions of microscopic red corpuscles which are the carriers of oxygen, and an even greater number of the white corpuscles, which are the body's scavengers, its defenders from invasion by outside germs.

There are certain outer portions of the body, such as nails and the scales of the skin, which are dead matter, produced by the body and pushed out from it and no longer nourished by the blood. But all the still living parts of the body are fed at every instant by the stream of life. Each cell in the body takes the fuel which it needs for its activities, and combines it with the oxygen brought by the red corpuscles; and when the task of power-production has been achieved, the cell puts back into the blood-stream, not merely the carbon dioxide, but many complex chemical products—ammonia, uric acid, and the "fatigue poisons," indol, phenol and skatol. The blood-stream bears these along, and delivers some to the sweat glands to be thrown out, and some to the kidneys, and the rest to the lungs.

All of this complicated mass of activities is in normal health perfectly regulated and timed by the nervous system. You lie down to sleep, and your muscles rest, and the vital activities slow up, your heart beats only faintly; but let something frighten you, and you sit up, and these faculties leap into activity, your heart begins to pound, driving a fresh supply of blood and vital energy. You jump up and run, and these organs all set to work at top speed. If they did not do so, your muscles would have no fresh energy; they would become paralyzed by the fatigue poisons, and you would be, as we say, exhausted.

All the rest of the body might be described as a shelter and accessory to the life-giving blood-stream; all the rest is the blood-stream's means of protecting itself and renewing itself. The stomach is to digest and prepare new blood material, the teeth are to crush it and grind it, the hands are to seize it, the eyes are to see it, the brain is to figure out its whereabouts. Man, in his egotism, imagines his little world as the center of the universe; but the wise old fellow who lives somewhere deep in our subconsciousness and looks after the welfare of our blood-stream—he has far better reason for believing that all our consciousness and our personality exist for him!

Now, disease is some failure of this blood-stream properly to renew itself or properly to protect itself and its various subsidiary organs. When you find yourself with a disease, you call in a doctor; and unless this doctor is a modern and progressive man, he makes the mistake of assuming that the disease is in the particular organ where it shows itself. You have, let us say, "follicular tonsilitis." (These medical men have a love for long names, which have the effect of awing you, and convincing you that you are in desperate need of attention.) Your throat is sore, your tonsils are swollen and covered with white spots; so the doctor hauls out his little black bag, and makes a swab of cotton and dips it, say in lysol, and paints your tonsils. He knows by means of the microscope that your tonsils are covered and filled with a mass of foreign germs which are feeding upon them; also he knows that lysol kills these germs, and he gives you a gargle for the same purpose, puts you to bed, and gradually the swelling goes down, and he tells you that he has cured you, and sends you a bill for services rendered. But maybe the swelling does not go down; maybe it gets worse and you die. Then he tells your family that nature was to blame. Nature is to blame for your death, but it never occurs to anyone to ask what nature may have had to do with your recovery.

I do not know how many thousands of diseases medical science has now classified. And for each separate disease there are complex formulas, and your system is pumped full of various mineral and vegetable substances which have been found to affect it in certain ways. Perhaps you have a fever; then we give you a substance which reduces the temperature of your blood-stream. It never occurs to us to reflect that maybe nature has some purpose of her own in raising the temperature of the blood; that this might be, so to speak, the heat of conflict, a struggle she is waging to drive out invading germs; and that possibly it would be better for the temperature to stay up until the battle is over. Or maybe the heart is failing; then our medical man is so eager to get something into the system that he cannot wait for the slow process of the mouth and the stomach, he shoots some strychnine directly into the blood-stream. It does not occur to him to reflect that maybe the heart is slowing up because it is overloaded with fatigue poisons, of which it cannot rid itself, and that the effect of stimulating it into fresh activity will be to leave it more dangerously poisoned than before.

We are dealing here with processes which our ancient mother nature has been carrying on for a long time, and which she very thoroughly understands. We ought, therefore, to be sure that we know what is the final effect of our actions; more especially we ought to be sure that we understand the cause of the evil, so that we may remove it, and not simply waste our time treating symptoms, putting plasters on a cancer. This is the fundamental problem of health; and in order to make clear what I mean, I am going to begin by telling a personal experience, a test which I made of medical science some twelve or fourteen years ago, in connection with one of the simplest and most external of the body's problems—the hair. First I will tell you what medical science was able to do for my hair, and second what I myself was able to do, when I put my own wits to work on the problem.

I had been overworking, and was in a badly run down condition. I was having headaches, insomnia, ulcerated teeth, many symptoms of a general breakdown; among these I noticed that my hair was coming out. I decided that it was foolish to become bald before I was thirty, and that I would take a little time off, and spend a little money and have my hair attended to. I did not know where to go, but I wanted the best authority available, so I wrote to the superintendent of the largest hospital in New York, asking him for the name of a reliable specialist in diseases of the scalp. The superintendent replied by referring me to a certain physician, who was the hospital's "consulting dermatologist," and I went to see this physician, whose home and office were just off Fifth Avenue.

He examined my scalp, and told me that I had dandruff in my hair, and that he would give me a prescription which would remove this dandruff and cause my hair to stop falling out. He charged me ten dollars for the visit, which in those days was more money than it is at present. Being of an inquiring turn of mind, I tried to get my money's worth by learning what there was to learn about the human hair. I questioned this gentleman, and he told me that the hair is a dead substance, and that its only life is in the root. He explained that barbers often persuade people to have their hair singed, to keep it from falling out, and that this was an utterly futile procedure, and likewise all shampooing and massage, which only caused the hair to fall out more quickly. It was better even not to wash the hair too often. All that was needed was a mixture of chemicals to kill the dandruff germs; and so I had the prescription put up at a drug store, and for a couple of years I religiously used it according to order, and it had upon my hair absolutely no effect whatever.

So here was the best that medical science could do. But still, I did not want to be bald, so I went among the health cranks—people who experiment without license from the medical schools. Also, I experimented upon myself, and now I know something about the human hair, something entirely different from what the rich and successful "consulting dermatologist" taught me, but which has kept me from becoming entirely bald:

First, the human hair is made by the body, and it is made, like everything else in the body, out of the blood-stream. It is perfectly true that the dandruff germ gets into the roots, and makes trouble, and that the process of killing this germ can be helped by chemicals; but it does not take a ten-dollar prescription, it only takes ten cents' worth of borax and salt from the corner grocery. (Put a little into a saucer, moisten it, rub it into the scalp, and wash it out again.) But infinitely more important than this is the fact that healthy hair roots are a product of healthy blood, and that unhealthy blood produces sick hair roots, which cannot hold in the hair. Most important of all is the fact that in order to make healthy hair roots the blood must flow fully and freely to these hair roots; whereas I had been accustomed for many hours every day of my life to clap around my scalp a tight band which almost entirely stopped the circulation of the life-giving blood to my sick hair roots. In other words, by wearing civilized hats, I was literally starving my hair to death.

As soon as I realized this I took off my civilized hat, and have never worn one since. As a rule, I don't wear anything. On the few occasions when I go into the city, I wear a soft cap. Now and then I experience inconvenience from this—the elevator boy in some apartment house tells me to come in by the delivery entrance, or the porter of a sleeping-car will not let me in at all. I remember discussing these embarrassments with Jack London, who went even further in his defiance of civilization, and wore a soft shirt. It was his custom, he said, to knock down the elevator boys and sleeping-car porters. I answered that that might be all right for him, because he could do it; whereas I was reduced to the painful expedient of explaining politely why I went about without the customary symbols of my economic superiority.

The "consulting dermatologist" had very solemnly and elaborately warned me concerning the danger of moving my hair too violently, and thus causing it to come out; but now my investigations brought out the fact that moving the hair, that is, massaging the scalp, increases the flow of blood to the hair roots, and further increases resistance to disease. As for causing the hair to fall out, I discovered that the more quickly you cause a hair to fall out, the greater is the chance of your getting another hair. If a hair is allowed to die in the root, it kills that root forever, but if it is pulled out before it dies, the root will make a new hair. Every "beauty parlor" specialist knows this; she knows that if a hair is pulled, it grows back bigger and stronger than ever, and so to pull out hair is the last thing you must do if you want to get rid of hairs!

I know a certain poet, who happens to have been well-endowed with physical graces by our mother nature. He finds it worth while to preserve them—they being accessory to those amorous experiences which form so large a part of the theme of poetry. Anyhow, this poet values his beautiful hair, and you will see him sitting in front of his fireplace, reading a book, and meanwhile his fingers run here and there over his head, and he grabs a bunch of hair and pulls and twists it. He has cultivated this habit for many years, and as a result his hair is as thick and heavy as the "fuzzy-wuzzies" of Kipling's poem. It is a favorite sport of this poet to lure some rival poet into a contest. He will mildly suggest that they take hold of each other's hair and have a tug of war. The rival poet, all unsuspecting, will accept the challenge, and my friend will proceed to haul him all over the place, to the accompaniment of howls of anguish from the victim, and howls of glee from the victor, who has, of course, a scalp as tough as a rhinoceros hide.

I am not a poet, and it is not important that I should be beautiful, and I have been too busy to remember to pull my hair; but by giving up tight hats, and by limiting the amount of my overworking, I have managed to keep what hair I had left when the hair specialist had got through with me. I tell this anecdote at the beginning of my discussion of health, because it illustrates so well the factors which appear in every case of disease, and which you must understand in seeking to remedy the trouble.

We have a phrase which has come down to us from the ancient Latins, "vis medicatrix naturae," which means the healing power of nature. So long ago men realized that it is our ancient mother who heals our wounds, and not the physician. Out of this have grown the cults of "nature cure" enthusiasts; and according to the fashion of men, they fly to extremes just as unreasonable and as dangerous as those of the "pill doctors" they are opposing. I have in mind a man who taught me probably more than any other writer on health questions, and with whom I once discussed the subject of typhoid, how it seemed to affect able-bodied men in the prime of their physical being. This, of course, was contrary to the theories of nature cure, and my friend had a simple way of meeting the argument—he refused to believe it. He insisted that, as with all other germ infections, it must be a question of bodily tone; no germ could secure lodgment in the human body unless the body's condition was reduced.

"But how can you be sure of that?" I argued. "You know that if you go into the jungle, you are not immune against the scorpion or the cobra or the tiger. There is nothing in all nature that is safe against every enemy. What possible right have you to assert that you are immune against every enemy which can attack your blood-stream?"

We shall find here, as we find nearly always, that the truth lies somewhere between the extremes of two warring schools. Our race has been existing for a long time in a certain environment, and its very existence implies superiority to that environment. The weaklings, for whom its hardships were too severe, were weeded out; hostile parasites invaded their blood-stream and conquered and devoured them. But those who survived were able to make in their blood-stream the substances known as anti-bodies, the "opsonins," to help the white blood corpuscles devour the germs. As the result of their victory, we carry those anti-bodies in our system, which gives us immunity to those particular diseases, or at any rate gives us the ability to have the diseases without dying. Every time we go into a street car, we take into our throat and lungs the germs of tuberculosis. Examination proves that we carry around with us in our mouths the germs of all the common throat and nose diseases, colds, bronchitis, tonsilitis. No matter what precautions we might take, no matter if we were to gargle our throats every few minutes, we could never get rid of such germs. And they wage continual war upon the body's defenses; they batter in vain upon the gates of our sound health. But take us to some new environment to which we are not accustomed; take us to Panama in the old days of yellow fever, or take us to Africa, and let the tsetse fly bite us, and infect us with "sleeping sickness." Here are germs to which our systems are not accustomed; and before them we are as helpless as the ancient knights-at-arms, who had conquered everything in sight, and ruled the continent of Europe for many hundreds of years, but were wiped off the earth by a chemist mixing gunpowder.

In the Marquesas Islands, in the South Seas, there lived a beautiful and happy race of savages, believed to have been descended, long ages ago, from Aryan stock. From the point of view of physical perfection, they were an ideal race, living a blissful outdoor life, which you may read about in Melville's "Typee," and in O'Brien's "White Shadows in the South Seas." This race conformed to all the requirements of the nature enthusiast. They went practically naked, their houses were open all the time, they lived on the abundant fruits of the earth. To be sure, they were cannibals, but this was more a matter of religious ceremony than of diet. They ate their war captives, but this was only after battle, and not often enough to count, one way or the other, in matters of health. They had lived for uncounted ages in perfect harmony with their environment; they were happy and free; and certainly, if such a thing were possible to human beings, they should have been proof against germs. But a ship came to one of these islands, and put ashore a sailor dying of tuberculosis, and in a few years four-fifths of the population of this island had been wiped out by the disease. What tuberculosis left were finished by syphilis and smallpox, and today the Marquesans are an almost extinct race.

But there is another side to the argument—and one more favorable to the nature cure enthusiast. We civilized men, by soft living, by self-indulgence and lack of exercise, may reduce the tone of our body too far below the standard which our ancestors set for us; and then the common disease germs get us, then we have colds, sore throats, tuberculosis. The nature cure advocate is perfectly right in saying that there is no use treating such diseases; the thing is to restore the body to its former tone, so that we may be superior to our normal environment and its strains.

You know the poem of the "One Hoss Shay," which was so perfectly built in every part that it ran for fifty years and then collapsed all at once in a heap. But the human body is not built that way. It always has one or more places which are weaker than the others, and which first show the effects of strain. In one person it will take the form of dyspepsia, in another it will be headaches, in another colds, in another decaying teeth, in another hardening of the arteries or stiffening of the joints. But whatever the symptoms may be, the fundamental cause is always the same, an abnormal condition of the blood-stream, and a consequent lowering of the body's tone. Therefore, studying any disease and its cure, you have first the emergency question, are there any germs lodged in the body, and if so, how can you destroy them? As part of the problem, you have to ask whether your blood-stream is normal, and if not, what are the methods by which you can make it normal and keep it so? Also you have to ask, what are the reasons why your trouble manifests itself in this or that particular organ? Is there some weakness or defect there, and can the defect be remedied, or can your habits be changed so as to reduce the strain on that organ? Are there any measures you can take to increase the flow of blood to that organ, and to promote its activity? In the study of your health, you will find that circumstances differ, and the importance of one factor or the other will vary; but you will seldom find any problem in which all these factors do not enter, and you will seldom find an adequate remedy unless you take all the factors into consideration.

CHAPTER XIX

EXPERIMENTS IN DIET

(Narrates the author's adventures in search of health, and his conclusions as to what to eat.)

Students of the body assure us that every particle of matter which composes it is changed in the course of seven years. It is obvious that everything that is a part of the body has at some time to be taken in as food; so the problem of our diet today is the problem of what our body shall consist of seven years from now, and probably a great deal sooner.

I begin this discussion by telling my own personal experiences with food. I am not going to recommend my diet for anyone else; because one of the first things I have to say about the subject is that every human individual is a separate diet problem. But I am going to try to establish a few principles for your guidance, and more especially to point out the commonest mistakes. I tell about my own mistakes, because it happens that I know them more intimately.

I was brought up in the South, where it is the custom of people to give a great deal of time and thought to the subject of eating. Among the people I knew it was always taken for granted that there should be at least one person in the kitchen devoting all her time to the preparing of delicious things for the family to eat. This person was generally a negress, and, needless to say, she knew nothing about the chemistry of foods, nothing about their constituents or nutritive qualities. All she knew was about their taste; she had been trained to prepare them in ways that tasted best, and was continually being advised and exhorted and sometimes scolded by the ladies of the family on this subject. At the table the family and the guests never failed to talk about the food and its taste, and not infrequently the cook would be behind the door listening to their comments; or else she would wait until after the meal, for the report which somebody would bring her.

In addition to this, the ladies of the family were skilled in what is called "fancy cooking." They did not bother with the meats and vegetables, but they mixed batter cakes, and made all kinds of elaborate desserts, and exchanged these treasures and the recipes for them with other ladies in the neighborhood. In addition to this, there were certain periods of the week and of the year especially devoted to the preparing and consuming of great quantities of foods. Once every seven days the members of the family expressed their worship of their Creator by eating twice as much as usual; and at another time they celebrated the birth of their Redeemer by overeating systematically for a period of two or three weeks. Needless to say, of course, the children brought up in such an environment all had large appetites and large stomachs, and their susceptibility to illness was recognized by the setting apart for them of a whole classification of troubles —"children's diseases," they were called. In addition to children's diseases, there were coughs and colds and sore throats and pains in the stomach and constipation and diarrhea, which the children shared with their adults.

I had a little more than my share of all these troubles. Always a doctor would be sent for, and always he was wise and impressive, and always I was impressed. He gave me some pills or a bottle of liquid, a teaspoonful every two hours, or something like that—I can hear the teaspoon rattle in the glass as I write. I had a profound respect for each and every one of those doctors. He was wisdom walking about in trousers, and whenever he came, I knew that I was going to get well; and I did, which proved the case completely.

Then I grew up, and at the age of eighteen or nineteen became possessed of a desire for knowledge, and took to reading and studying literally every minute of the day and a good part of the night. I seldom let myself go to sleep before two o'clock in the morning, and was always up by seven and ready for work again. I did this for ten years or so, until nature brought me to a complete stop. During these ten years I was a regular experiment station in health; that is, I had every kind of common ailment, and had it over and over again, so that I could try all the ways of curing it, or failing to cure it, and keep on trying until I was sure, one way or the other. I came recently upon a wonderful saying by John Burroughs, which will be appreciated by every author. "This writing is an unnatural business. It makes your head hot and your feet cold, and it stops the digesting of your food."

This trouble with my digestion began when I was writing my second novel, camping out on a lonely island at the foot of Lake Ontario. I went to see a doctor in a nearby town, and he talked learnedly about dyspepsia. The cause of it, he said, was failure of the stomach to secrete enough pepsin, and the remedy was to take artificial pepsin, obtained from the stomach of a pig. He gave me this pig-pepsin in a bottle of red liquid, and I religiously took some after each meal. It helped for a time; but then I noticed that it helped less and less. I got so that a simple meal of cold meat and boiled potatoes would stay in my stomach for hours, in spite of any amount of the pig-pepsin; I would lie about in misery, because I wanted to work, and my accursed stomach would not let me.

All the time, of course, I was using my mind on this problem, groping for causes. I found that the trouble was worse if I worked immediately after eating. I found also that it was worse when I was writing books. When I got sufficiently desperate, I would stop writing books and go off on a hunting trip. I would tramp twenty miles a day over the mountains, looking for deer, and I would come back at night too tired to think, and in a week or two every trace of my trouble would be gone. So my life regimen came to be— first the writing of a book, and then a hunting trip to get over the effects of it. But as time went on, alas, I noticed that the recuperation was more slow and less certain. The working times grew shorter, and the hunting times grew longer, until finally I had got to a point where I couldn't work at all; I would go to pieces in a few days if I tried it. It was apparently the end of my stomach, and the end of my sleeping, and the end of my writing books. My teeth were decaying, not merely outside but inside; I would have abscesses, and most frightful agonies to endure. I would lie awake all night, and it would seem to me that I could feel my body going to pieces—an extremely depressing sensation!

I had been trying experiments all this time. I had been going to one doctor after another, and had got to realize that the doctors only treated symptoms; they treated the "diseases" when they appeared—but nobody ever told you how to keep the "diseases" from appearing. Why could there not be a doctor who would look you over thoroughly, and tell you everything that was wrong with you, and how to set it right? A doctor who would tell you exactly how to live, so that you might keep well all the time! I was studying economics, and becoming suspicious of my fellow man; it occurred to me that possibly it might be embarrassing to a doctor, if he cured all his patients, and taught them how to live, so that none of them would ever have to come to him again. It occurred to me that possibly this might be the reason why "preventive medicine," constructive health work, was getting so little attention from the medical fraternity.

Two things that plagued me were headache and constipation, and they were obviously related. For constipation, the world had one simple remedy; you "took something" every night or every morning, and thought no more about it. My stout and amiable grandmother had drunk a glass of Hunyadi water every morning for the last thirty or forty years, and that she finally died of "fatty degeneration of the heart" was not connected with this in the mind of anyone who knew her. As for the headaches, people would tell you this, that, and the other remedy, and I would try them—that is, unless they happened to be drugs. I was getting more and more shy of drugs. I had some blessed instinct which saved me from stimulants and narcotics. I had never used tea, coffee, alcohol or tobacco, and in my worst periods of suffering I never took to putting myself to sleep with chloral, or to stopping my headaches with phenacetin.

At the end of six or eight years of purgatory, I came upon a prospectus of the Battle Creek Sanitarium. This seemed to me exactly what I wanted; this was constructive, it dealt with the body as a whole. So I spent a couple of months at the "San," and paid them something like a thousand dollars to tell me all they could about myself.

The first thing they told me was that meat-eating was killing me. It was perfectly obvious, was it not, that meat is a horrible feeding place for germs, that rotten meat is dreadfully offensive, and likewise digested meat —consider the excreta of cats, for example! I listened solemnly while Doctor Kellogg read off the numbers of billions of bacteria per gram in the contents of the colon of a carnivorous person. It certainly seemed proper that the author of "The Jungle" should be a vegetarian, so I became one, and did my best to persuade myself that I enjoyed the taste of the patent meat-substitutes which are served in hundred calory portions in the big Sanitarium dining-room.

There also I met Horace Fletcher, and learned to chew every particle of food thirty-two times, and often more. I exercised in the Sanitarium gymnasium, and watched the sterilized dancing—the men with the men and the women with the women. I was patiently polite with the Seventh Day Adventist religion, and laid in a supply of postage stamps on Friday evening. Finally, and most important of all, I went once a day to the "treatment rooms," and had my abdomen doctored alternately with hot cloths and ice. By this means I kept up a flow of blood in the intestinal tract, and stimulated these organs to activity; so my constipation was relieved, and my headaches were less severe—so long as I stayed at the Sanitarium, and was boiled and frozen once every day. But when I left the Sanitarium, and abandoned the treatments, the troubles began to return. Meantime, however, I had written a book in praise of vegetarianism—a book which has got into the libraries, and cannot be got out again!

I went on to a new variety of health crank, the real "nature cure" practitioners. Vegetarianism was not enough, they insisted; the evil had begun long before, when man first ruined his food and destroyed its nutritive value by means of fire. There was only one certain road to health, and that was by the raw food route, the monkey and squirrel diet. I had gone out to California for a winter's rest, and decided I would give this plan a thorough trial. For five months I lived by myself, and the only cooked food I ate was shredded wheat biscuit. For the rest I lived on nuts and salads and fresh and dried fruits; and during this period I enjoyed such health as I had never known in my life before. I had literally not a single ailment. I was not merely well, but bubbling over with health. I had a friend who said it cheered him up just to see me walk down the street.

I thought that it was entirely the raw food, and that I had solved the problem forever; but I overlooked the fact that during those five months I had done no hard brain work, no writing. I went back to writing again, and things began to go wrong; my wonderful raw foods took to making trouble in my stomach—and I assure you that until you try, you have no idea the amount of trouble that can be made in your stomach by a load of bananas and soaked prunes which has gone wrong! For a year or two I agonized; I could not give up my wonderful raw food diet, because I had always before me the vision of those months in California, and could not understand why it was not that way again.

But the time came when I would eat a meal of raw food, and for hours afterwards my stomach would feel like a blown-up football. Then somebody gave me a book by Dr. Salisbury on the subject of the meat diet. Of all the horrible things in the world, a meat diet sounded to me the worst; I had been a vegetable enthusiast for three years, and thought of eating meat as you would think of cannibalism. But there has never been a time in my life when I would not hear something new, and give it a trial if it sounded well; so I read the books of Doctor Salisbury, which have long been out of print, and have been curiously neglected by the medical profession. Salisbury was a real pioneer, an experimenter. He wrote in the days before the germ theory, and so missed his guess regarding tuberculosis, but he perceived that most of the common diseases are caused by dietetic errors, and he set to work to prove it. He showed that hog cholera and army diarrhea are the same disease, and come from the same cause. He took a squad of men and fed them on army biscuit for two or three weeks, until they were nearly dead, and then he put them on a diet of lean beef and completely cured them in a few days. He did this same thing with one kind of food after another, and in each case he would bring his men as near to death as he dared, and then he would cure them. He showed that meat is the only food which contains all the elements of nutrition, the only food upon which a person can live for an unlimited period. As Salisbury said, "Beef is first, mutton is second, and the rest nowhere."

It was his idea that tuberculosis of the lungs is caused by spores of fermenting starch clogging the minute blood vessels. He claimed that there is an early stage of tuberculosis, in which the spores are floating in the blood stream; he put large numbers of patients upon a diet of lean beef, ground and cooked, and he cured them of tuberculosis, and if one of them would break the diet and yield to a craving for starch or sugar, Salisbury claimed that he could find it out an hour or two later by examining a drop of their blood under the microscope. In his books he described vividly the effects of an excess of starch and sugar in the diet. He called it "making a yeast-pot of your stomach"; and you can imagine how that hit my stomach, full of half digested bananas and prunes!

I tried the Salisbury diet, and satisfied myself of this one fact, that lean meat is for brain-workers the most easily assimilated of all foods. Salisbury claimed that you could not overeat on meat, but I do not believe there is any food you cannot overeat on, nor do I believe that anyone should try to live on one kind of food. We are by nature omnivorous animals. Our digestive tracts are similar to those of hogs and monkeys, which eat all varieties of food they can get. One of the common errors of the nature cure enthusiast is to cite the monkey and the squirrel as fruit and nut-eating animals, when the fact is that monkeys and squirrels eat meat when they can get it, and the ardor with which they go bird-nesting is evidence enough that they crave it. If there is any race of man which is vegetarian, you will find that it is from necessity alone. The beautiful South Sea Islanders, who are the theme of the raw fooders' ecstasy, spend a lot of their time catching fish, and sometimes they kill a pig, and celebrate the event precisely as Christians celebrate the birth of their Redeemer.

From this you may be able to guess my conclusions, as the result of much painful blundering and experimenting. So far as diet is concerned, I belong to no school; I have learned something from each one, and what I have learned from a trial of them all is to be shy of extreme statements and of hard and fast rules. To my vegetarian friends who argue that it is morally wrong to take sentient life, I answer that they cannot go for a walk in the country without committing that offense, for they walk on innumerable bugs and worms. We cannot live without asserting our right to subject the lower forms of life to our purposes; we kill innumerable germs when we swallow a glass of grape juice, or for that matter a glass of plain water. I shall be much surprised if the advance of science does not some day prove to us that there are rudimentary forms of consciousness in all vegetable life; so we shall justify the argument of Mr. Dooley, who said, in reviewing "The Jungle," that he could not see how it was any less a crime to cut off a young tomato in its prime, or to murder a whole cradleful of baby peas in the pod!

There is no question that meat-eating is inconvenient, expensive, and dirty. I have no doubt that some day we shall know enough to be able to find for every individual a diet which will keep him at the top of his power, without the maintenance of the slaughter-house. But we do not possess that knowledge at present; at least, I personally do not possess it. I happen to be one of those individuals—there are many of them—with whom milk does not agree; and if you rule out milk and meat, you find yourself compelled to get a great deal of your protein from vegetable sources, such as peas, beans and nuts. All these contain a great deal of starch, and thus there is no way you can arrange your diet to escape an excess of starch. Excess of starch, so my experience has convinced me, is the deadliest of all dietetic errors. It is also the commonest of errors, the cause, not merely of the common throat and nose infections, but of constipation, and likewise of diarrhea, of anemia, and thus, through the weakening of the blood stream, of all disorders that spring from this source—decaying teeth and rheumatism, boils, bad complexion, and tuberculosis. Starch foods are the cheapest, therefore they form the common diet of the poor, and are responsible for the diseases of undernourishment to which the poor are liable.

On the other hand, of course, there are perfectly definite diseases of overnourishment; high blood pressure, which culminates in apoplexy; kidney troubles, which result from the inability of these organs to eliminate all the waste matter that is delivered to them; fatty degeneration of the heart, or of the liver, or any of the vital organs. You may cause a headache by clogging the blood stream through overeating, or you may cause it by eating small quantities of food, if those foods are unbalanced, and do not contain the mineral elements necessary to the making of normal blood. Whatever the trouble with your health, it is my judgment that in two cases out of three you will find it dates back to errors in diet. I do not think I exaggerate in saying that a knowledge of what to eat and how much to eat is two-thirds of the knowledge of how to keep yourself in permanent health.

CHAPTER XX

ERRORS IN DIET

(Discusses the different kinds of foods, and the part they play in the making of health and disease.)

It is my purpose in this chapter to lay down a few general principles to aid you in the practical problem of selecting the best diet for yourself. But it must be made clear at the outset that there can be no hard and fast rule. All human bodies are more or less alike, but on the other hand all are more or less different. Modern civilization has given very few bodies the chance to be perfect; nearly all have some weakness, some abnormality, and need some special modification in diet to fit their particular problem. The ideal in each case would be a complete study of the individual system. Some day, no doubt, medical science will analyze the digestive juices and the gland secretions and the blood-stream of every human being, and say, you need a certain percentage of starch and a certain percentage of protein; you need such and such proportion of phosphorus and iron; you should avoid certain acids—and so on. But at present we are devoting our science to the task of killing and maiming other people, instead of enabling ourselves to live in health and happiness; so it is that most of those who read this book will be too poor to command the advice of a diet specialist. The best you can do is to get a few general ideas and try them out, watching your own body and learning its peculiarities.

Human food contains three elements: proteins, fats and carbohydrates. The proteins are the body-building material, and the foods which are rich in proteins are lean meat, the white of eggs, milk and cheese, nuts, peas and beans. A certain amount of this kind of food is needed by the body. If it is missing, the body will gradually waste away. If too much of it is taken, the body can turn it into energy-making material, but this is a wasteful process, and the best evidence appears to be that it is a strain upon the system. Experiments conducted by Professor Chittenden of Yale have proven conclusively that men can live and maintain body weight upon much less protein food than previous dietetic standards had indicated.

The fats are found in fat meats and dairy products, and in nuts, olives, and vegetable oils. The body is prepared to digest and assimilate a certain amount of fat, no one knows how much. I have found in my own case that I require a great deal less than people ordinarily eat. I have for many years maintained good health upon a diet containing no more fat than one gets with lean meat once or twice a day. I never use butter or olive oil, nor any fat in cooking. My reason for this is that fats are the most highly concentrated form of food, and the easiest upon which to overeat. Excess of fat is a cause, not merely of obesity, but also of boils and pimples and "pasty" complexion, and other signs of a clogged blood-stream.

The third variety of food is the carbohydrates, and of these there are two kinds, starches and sugars. Starch is the white material of the grains and tubers; the principal food element of bread and cereals, rice, potatoes, bananas, and many prepared substances such as corn-starch, tapioca, farina and macaroni. Starchy foods compose probably half the diet of the average human being. In my own case, they compose about one-sixth, so you see to what extent my beliefs differ from the common. Starch is not really necessary in the diet at all. I have a friend who is subject to headaches, and finds relief from them by a diet of meat, salads, and fresh fruits exclusively. The first thing that excess of starch or sugar does is to ferment in the system, and cause flatulence and gas. But strange as it may seem, if the excess of starch is perfectly digested and assimilated into the system, the condition may be worse yet, because you may have a great quantity of energy-producing material, without the necessary mineral elements which the body requires in the handling of it.

If you cremate a human body and study the ashes chemically, you find a score or more of mineral salts. You find these in the blood, and no blood is normal and no body can be kept normal which does not contain the right percentage of these elements. It is not merely that they are needed to build bones and teeth; they are needed at every instant for the chemistry of the cells. Every time you move a muscle, you fill the cells of that muscle with a certain amount of waste matter. You may prove how deadly this matter is by binding a tight cord about your arm, and then trying to use the arm. We are only at the beginning of understanding the subtle chemistry of the body; but this much we know, the cells transform the waste products, and they are thrown out of the system as ammonia, uric acid, etc.; and for this process the blood must have a continual supply of many mineral salts.

So vital are they, and so fatal to health is their absence, that it is far better for you to eat nothing at all than to eat improperly balanced foods, or foods which are deficient in the organic salts. You may prove this to yourself by a simple experiment. Put two chickens in separate pens, where nobody can feed them but yourself. Feed one of them on water and white bread, or corn starch, or sugar, or any energy-making substance which contains little of the mineral elements. Feed the other chicken on plain water. You will find that the one which has the food will quickly become droopy and sickly; its feathers will fall out, it will have what in human beings would be known as headaches, colds, sore throats, decaying teeth and boils. At the end of a couple of weeks it will be a dead chicken. The one which you feed on water alone will not be a happy chicken, neither will it be a fat chicken, but it will be a live chicken, and a chicken without disease. I am going later on to discuss the subject of fasting. For the present I will merely say that a chicken which has nothing but water is living upon its own flesh, and therefore has a meat diet, containing the mineral elements necessary to the elimination of the fatigue poisons.

I am going to try not to be dogmatic in this book, and not to say things that I do not know. I confess to innumerable uncertainties about the subject of diet; but one thing I think I do know, and that is that human beings should eliminate absolutely from their food those modern artificial products, which look so nice, and are so easy to handle, and are put up in packages with pretty labels, and have been in some way artificially treated to remove the wastes and impurities—including the vital mineral salts. Among such food substances I include lard and its imitations made from cottonseed oil, white flour, all the prepared and refined cereals, polished rice, tapioca, farina, corn starch, and granulated and powdered sugar. Any of these substances will kill a chicken in a couple of weeks, and the only reason they take a longer time to kill you is because you mix them with other kinds of foods. But to the extent that you eat them, your diet is deficient; and do not console yourself with the idea that the mineral elements will be made up from other foods, because you don't know that, and nobody else knows it. Nobody knows just how much of any particular organic salt the body needs. All we know is that the primitive races, which ate natural foods, enjoyed vigorous health, while the American people, who consume the greatest proportion of the so-called "refined" foods, have the very best dentists and the very worst teeth in the world.

There are many kinds of sugar, found in the sugar-cane and the beet, and in all fruits. Sugar may also be made from any form of starch; this is glucose, which is put up in cans and sold as an imitation of maple syrup. The ordinary granulated and powdered sugar is made by taking from the natural syrup every trace of mineral elements; so I have no hesitation in saying that the ordinary cane sugar and beet sugar of our breakfast tables and our confectionery stores is not a food, but a slow poison. The causes of the wonderful progress of American dentistry, which is the marvel of the civilized world, are cane sugar, white flour, and the frying-pan, each of which dietetic crimes I shall take up in turn.

We have the richest country in the world; we eat more food, probably by 50 per cent, and we waste more food, probably by 500 per cent, than any other people in the world; and yet, go to any small farming community in America, and what do you find? You find the teeth of the young children rotting in their heads, and having to be pulled out before their second teeth come. You find these second teeth rotting often before the age of twenty. A friend of mine, who knows the American farmer, sums it up this way: "He has two things that he requires if he is to be really respectable and happy. First, he wants to get all the fireplaces in his home boarded up, and all the windows nailed tight; and second, he wants to get all his teeth out, and an artificial set installed. Out of the farmers' wives in my neighborhood, not one in ten keeps her own teeth until she is thirty."

If you go to the Balkans, where the peasants live on sour milk, with grains which they grind at home; or to southern Italy and Sicily, where they live on cheese and black bread and olives; or among savage people, where they hunt and fish and gather the natural fruits, you find old men without a single decayed tooth. There must be some reason for this, and the reason is found in our denatured grocery-store foods. The farmer's wife will gather up her eggs and her butter and cheeses, and take them to the store and bring back cans of lard and packages of sugar. The farmer will sell his perfectly good wheat and corn meal, and bring back in his wagon cases of "refined" cereal foods, for which he has paid ten times the price of the grain!

Dentists will tell you that the way candy injures the teeth is by sticking to them and fermenting, forming acids, which destroy the tooth structure. And that may be a part of the reason. But the principal reason why the teeth decay is because the blood-stream is abnormal, and is unable to keep up the repairs of the body. Your teeth are living structures, just as much as any other part of you, and they will resist decay if you supply them with the proper nourishment.

You need sugar; you need a considerable quantity of it every day. Nature provides this sugar in combination with the organic salts, and also with the precious vitamines, whose function in the body we are only beginning to investigate. All the mineral substances which give the color and flavor to oranges, apples, peaches, grapes, figs, prunes, raisins—all these you take out when you make sugar. Or perhaps you put in some imitations of them, made from coal tar chemicals, and drink them at your soda fountains! So little appreciation has the American farmer's wife of natural fruits, that when she preserves them, she considers it necessary to fill them full of cane sugar; in fact, she has a notion that they won't keep unless she cooks them up with sugar! So snobbish are we Americans about our eating, that we make the best of our foods into bywords. We make jokes in our comic papers about the "boarding-house prune"; and yet prunes and raisins are among the wholesomest foods we have, and if we fed them to our children instead of cakes and candy and coal-tar flavorings, our dental industry would rapidly decline.

And the same thing is true of bread. When I was a boy, I thought I had to have hot bread at least twice a day, and if I were called upon to eat bread that was more than a day old, I felt that I was being badly abused by life. I used to read fairy stories, in which something called "black bread" was mentioned, something obscure and terrible; the symbol of human misery was Cinderella sitting in the ashes and eating a crust of dry "black bread." But now since I have studied diet, I have taken my place with Cinderella. I can afford to buy whatever kind of bread I want; I can have the best white bread, piping hot, three times a day, if I want it; but what I eat three times a day is a crust of hard dry "black bread."

"Black bread" is the fairy story name for bread made of the whole grain. It is eaten that way by the peasant because he has no patent milling machinery at his disposal, to fan away the life-giving elements of his food. Nearly all the mineral elements of the grain are contained in the outer, dark-colored portion. The white part is almost pure starch; and when you use white flour, you are not merely starving your blood-stream, your bones, and your teeth, you are also depriving the digestive tract of the rough material which it is accustomed to handle, and which it needs to stimulate it to action. I am aware that whole grain products are a trifle less easy of digestion, but we should not pamper and weaken our digestive tract any more than we let our muscles get flabby for lack of action. We should require our stomachs to handle the ordinary natural foods, precisely as we accustom our body to react from cold water, and to stand honest hard work.

For ages the Japanese peasants have lived on rice, with a little dried fish. Quite recently there began to spread throughout Japan a mysterious disease known as beri-beri. It was especially prevalent in the army, and so the scientists of Japan set out to discover the cause, and it proved to be the modern practice of polishing rice, which takes off the outer coating of the grain. Rice is one of the most wholesome of foods, if it is eaten in the natural state; but in order to get it in that state in this country, you have to find a special food store of the health cranks, and have to pay a special price for it. You have to pay a higher price for whole wheat bread—because ninety-nine people out of a hundred are ignorant, and insist upon having their foodstuffs pretty to look at!

Probably you have read sea stories, and know of the horrors of scurvy. Scurvy and beri-beri are similar diseases, with a similar cause. The men on the old sailing ships used to have to live on white biscuit and salt meat, and they always knew that to recover from their gnawing illness, they must get to port and get fresh vegetables and fruits, especially onions and lemons, which contain the vitamines as well as the salts. But you will see the modern housewife going into the grocery store, and surveying the shelves of "package" goods, and in her ignorance picking out the scurvy-making products, and frequently paying for them a much higher price than for the health-making ones!

Then, when she has got her white flour, and her cane sugar, and her lard, she will take it home, and mix it up, and put it in the frying pan, and serve it hot to her husband and children. Nature has so constituted her husband and children that they digest starch before they digest fat; that is to say, the starch is digested mainly in the stomach, while the fat is digested mainly after the food has been passed on into the small intestine. But by frying the starch before it is eaten, the housewife carefully takes each grain of the starch and protects it with a little covering of fat. Thus the digestive juices of the stomach cannot get at the starch, and the starch goes down into the small intestine a good part undigested. If some evil spirit, wishing to make trouble for the human organism, had charge of the laying out of our diet, he could hardly devise anything worse than that. And yet it would be no exaggeration to say that the average American, especially the average farmer, eats out of a frying-pan. If his potatoes have to be warmed over, they go into the frying-pan; his precious batter-cakes and doughnuts are cooked in a frying-pan, and all his precious hot breads are mixed with lard. If it were not for the fact that you cannot broil a beefsteak over a modern gas range, I would tell you that the first step toward health for the average American would be to throw the frying-pan out of the window, and to throw the cook-book after it.

The whole modern art of cooking is largely a perversion; a product of idleness, vanity, and sensuality. It is one of the monstrous growths consequent upon our system of class exploitation. We have a number of idle people with nothing to do but eat, and who demonstrate their superiority to the rest of us by their knowledge of superior foods, and superior ways of preparing them. They have the wealth of the world at their disposal, also the services of their fellow man without limit, and they set their fellow man to work to enable them to give elaborate banquets, and to sit in solemn state and gorge themselves, and to have a full account of their behavior published in the next morning's newspapers. A great part of this perverse art we owe to what is called the "ancient régime" in France—a régime which starved the French peasantry until they were black skinned beasts hiding in caves and hollow trees. So it comes about that our modern food depravity parades itself in French names, and American snobbery requires of its devotees a course in the French language sufficient to read a menu card. Needless to say, this elaborate gastronomic art has been developed without any relation to health, or any thought of the true needs of the body. It is one of the products of the predatory system which we can say is absolute waste. Having done my own cooking for the past twenty-five years, I make bold to say that I can teach anybody all he needs to know about cooking in one lesson of half an hour, and that the total amount of cooking required for a large family can be done by one person in twenty minutes a day.

In the first place, a great many foods do not have to be cooked at all, and are made less fit by cooking. In the next place, the only cooking that is ever required is a little boiling, or in the case of meat, roasting or broiling. In the next place, the art of combining foods in cooking is a waste art, because no foods should be combined in cooking. Every food has its own natural flavor, which is lost in combination, and if anybody is unable to enjoy the natural flavors of simply cooked foods, there is one thing to say to that person, and that is to wait until he is hungry. Let him take a ten-mile walk in the open air, and he will have more interest in his next meal. I am not a fanatic, and have no desire to destroy the pleasures of life; I am recommending to people that they should seek the higher pleasures of the intellect, and those pleasures are not found in standing over a cook stove, nor in compelling others to stand over a cook stove. Moreover, I know that the artificial mixing of foods to tempt peoples' palates is one of the principal causes of overeating, and therefore of ill health, and therefore of the ultimate destruction of the pleasures of life.

I went out from the world of cooks before I was twenty. I wanted to write a book, and to be let alone while I was doing it. I lived by myself, and found out about cooking by practical experience. On a few occasions since then, I have lived in a house with a servant, and had some cooking done for me, but it was always because somebody else wanted it, and against my protest. In the last ten years we have had no servant in our home, and because I want my wife to give her energy to more important things than feeding me, I do my share of getting every meal. We have worked out a system of housekeeping by which we get a meal in five minutes, and when we finish it, it takes three minutes to clear things away.

If I tell you what I eat, please do not get the impression that I am advising you to eat these same things. My diet consists of the foods which I have found by long experience agree with me. There are many other foods which are just as wholesome, but which I do not eat, either because they don't happen to agree with me, or because I don't care for them so much. I am fond of fruit, and eat more of that than of anything else. It is not a cheap article of diet, but you can save a good deal if you buy it in quantities, as I do. A little later I am going to discuss the prices of foods.

For breakfast I eat a slice of whole wheat bread, three good-sized apples, stewed, and eight or ten dates. It takes practically no time to prepare this breakfast. The bread has to be baked, of course, but this is done wholesale; we buy four loaves at a time, and it is just as good at the end of a couple of weeks as when we buy it. When I lived in the world of cooks, I would call for apple sauce; which meant that somebody had to pare apples, cut them up, stew them, mix them with sugar, grate a little nutmeg over them, set them on ice, and serve them to me on a glass dish, with a little pitcher of cream. But now what happens is that I put a dozen apples in a big sauce-pan and let them simmer while I am eating. We have a rule in our family that we do not do any cooking except while we are eating, because if we try it at any other time of the day, we get buried in a book or in a manuscript, and forget about it until the smoke causes somebody in the street to summon the fire department. So the apples for my breakfast were cooked during last night's supper; and during the breakfast there will be some vegetable cooking for lunch.

At this lunch, which is my "square meal," I eat a large slice of beefsteak, say a third of a pound. Jack London used to say that the only man who could cook a beefsteak was the fireman of a railway locomotive, because he had a hot, clean shovel. The best imitation you can get is a hot, clean frying-pan; and when you are sure that it is hot, let it get hotter. The whole secret of cooking meat is to keep the juices inside, and to do that you must cook it quickly. When you slap it down on a hot frying-pan, the meat is seared, and the juices stay inside, and if you do not turn it over until it is almost ready to burn, you don't need to cook it very long on the other side. That is the one secret of cooking worth knowing; it doesn't cost anything, and saves time instead of wasting it. As I have never found anybody else capable of learning it, I reserve the cooking of the beefsteak as one of my family duties.

To continue the lunch, a slice of whole wheat bread, and a large quantity of some fresh salad, such as celery, or lettuce and tomatoes, without dressing. For a part of this may be substituted a vegetable, one or two beets or turnips, cooked during a previous meal, and warmed up in a couple of minutes; and we do not throw away the tops of the turnips and beets and celery, we put them on and cook them, and they serve for the next day's meal. If you would eat a large quantity of such "greens" once a day, you would escape many of the ills that your flesh is at present heir to. Finally, for dessert, an orange and a small handful of raisins, or one or two figs.

The evening meal will be the same as the breakfast; except once in a while when I am especially hungry, and want some meat. I am writing in the winter season, so the fruits suggested are those available in winter. The menu will be varied with every kind of fruit at the season when it is cheapest and most easily obtained. The beefsteak will appear at about three meals out of four; occasionally it will be replaced by the lean meat of pork or mutton, or by fish. The bread may be replaced by rice, or boiled potatoes, either white or sweet, and occasionally by graham crackers. I know that these contain a little fat and sugar, but I try not to be fanatical about my diet, and the rules I suggest do not carry the death penalty. There was a time when I used to allow my friends to make themselves miserable by trying to provide me with special foods when they invited me to a meal, but now I tell them to "forget it," and I politely nibble a little of everything, and eat most of what I find wholesome; if there is nothing wholesome, I content myself with the pretense of a meal. If I find myself in a restaurant, I quite shamelessly get a piece of apple or pumpkin pie, omitting most of the crust. As I don't go away from home more than once or twice a month, I do not have to worry about such indulgence. The main thing is to arrange one's home diet on sound lines, and learn to enjoy the simple and wholesome foods, of which there is a great variety obtainable, and at prices possible to all but the wretchedly poor.

In conclusion, since everybody likes to have a feast now and then, I specify that my diet regimen allows for holidays. Assuming that I am your guest for a day, and that you wish to "blow" me, regardless of expense, here will be the menu. Breakfast, some graham crackers, a bunch of raisins, a can of sliced pineapple in winter, or a big chunk of watermelon in summer. Dinner, or lunch, roast pork, a baked apple, a baked sweet potato and some spinach. Supper, lettuce, dates, and a dish of popcorn flavored with peanut butter. Try this next Christmas!

P. S. After this book had been put into type, I chanced to be looking over Herbert Quick's illuminating book, "On Board the Good Ship Earth." Discussing the importance of certain organic salts to the body, Dr. Quick states: "Animals have been fed, as an experiment, on foods deficient in phosphorus. For a while they seemed to do well. Then they collapsed. It takes only three months of a ration without phosphorus to wreck an animal. Individual creatures were killed after a month of this diet, and it was found that the flesh was taking the phosphate—for the phosphorus exists in the body in that form—from the bones to supply its need. In other words, the body was eating its own bones! When this process had robbed the bones to the limit, the collapse came, and the animal could never recover."

CHAPTER XXI

DIET STANDARDS

(Discusses various foods and their food values, the quantities we need, and their money cost.)

I think there is no more important single question about health than the question of how much food we should eat. It is one about which there is a great deal of controversy, even among the best authorities. We shall try here for a common-sense solution. At the outset we have to remind ourselves of the distinction we tried to draw between nature and man. To what extent can civilized man rely upon his instincts to keep him in perfect health?

Let us begin by considering the animals. How is their diet problem solved? Horses and cattle in a wild state are adjusted to certain foods which they find in nature, and so long as they can find it, they have no diet problem. Man comes, and takes these animals and domesticates them; he observes their habits, and gives to them a diet closely approaching the natural one, and they get along fairly well. But suppose the man, with his superior skill in agriculture, taking wild grain and planting it, reaping and threshing it by machinery, puts before his horse an unlimited quantity of a concentrated food such as oats, which the horse can never get in a natural state—will that horse's instincts guide it? Not at all. Any horse will kill itself by overeating on grain.

I have read somewhere a clever saying, that a farm is a good place for an author to live, provided he can be persuaded not to farm it. But once upon a time I had not heard that wise remark, and I owned and tried to run a farm. I had two beautiful cows of which I was very proud, and one morning I woke up and discovered that the cows had got into the pear orchard and had been feeding on pears all night. In a few hours they both lay with bloated stomachs, dying. A farmer told me afterwards that I might have saved their lives, if I had stuck a knife into their stomachs to let out the gas. I do not know whether this is true or not. But my two dead cows afford a perfect illustration of the reason why civilized man cannot rely upon his instincts and his appetites to tell him when he has had enough to eat. He can only do this, provided he rigidly restricts himself to the foods which he ate in the days when his teeth and stomach and bowels were being shaped by the process of natural selection. If he is going to eat any other than such strictly natural foods, he will need to apply his reason to his diet schedule.

In a state of nature man has to hunt his food, and the amount that he finds is generally limited, and requires a lot of exercise to get. Explorers in Africa give us a picture of man's life in the savage state, guided by his instincts and very little interfered with by reason. The savages will starve for long periods, then they will succeed in killing a hippopotamus or a buffalo, and they will gorge themselves, and nearly all of them will be ill, and several of them will die. So you see, even in a state of nature, and with natural foods, restraint is needed, and reason and moral sense have a part to play.

What do reason and moral sense have to tell us about diet? Our bodily processes go on continuously, and we need at regular intervals a certain quantity of a number of different foods. The most elementary experiment will convince us that we can get along, maintain our body weight and our working efficiency upon a much smaller quantity of food than we naturally crave. Civilized custom puts before us a great variety of delicate and appetizing foods, upon which we are disposed to overeat; and we are slow observers indeed if we do not note the connection between this overeating and ill health. So we are forced to the conclusion that if we wish to stay well, we need to establish a censorship over our habits; we need a different diet regimen from the haphazard one which has been established for us by a combination of our instincts with the perversions of civilization.

Up to a few years ago, it was commonly taken for granted by authorities on diet that what the average man actually eats must be the normal thing for him to eat. Governments which were employing men in armies, and at road building, and had to feed them and keep them in health, made large scale observations as to what the men ate, and thus were established the old fashioned "diet standards." They are expressed in calories, which is a heat unit representing the quantity of fuel required to heat a certain small quantity of water a certain number of degrees. In order that you may know what I am talking about, I will give a rough idea of the quantity of the more common foods which it takes to make 100 calories: one medium sized slice of bread, a piece of lean cooked steak the size of two fingers, one large apple, three medium tablespoonfuls of cooked rice or potatoes, one large banana, a tablespoonful of raisins, five dates, one large fig, a teaspoonful of sugar, a ball of butter the size of your thumbnail, a very large head of lettuce, three medium sized tomatoes, two-thirds of a glass of milk, a tablespoonful of oil. You observe, if you compare these various items, how little guidance concerning food is given by its bulk. You may eat a whole head of lettuce, weighing nearly a pound, and get no more food value than from a half ounce of olive oil which you pour over it. You may eat enough lean beefsteak to cover your plate, and you will not have eaten so much as a generous helping of butter. A big bowl of strawberries will not count half so much as the cream and sugar you put over them. So you may realize that when you eat olive oil, butter, cream, and sugar, you are in the same danger as the horse eating oats, or as my two cows in the pear orchard; and if some day a surgeon has to come and stick a knife into you, it may be for the same reason.

The old-fashioned diet standards are as follows: Swedish laborers at hard work, over 4,700 calories; Russian workmen at moderate work, German soldiers in active service, Italian laborers at moderate work, between 3,500 and 3,700 calories; English weavers, nearly 3,500 calories; Austrian farm laborers, over 5,000 calories. Some twenty years ago the United States government made observations of over 15,000 persons, and established the following, known as the "Atwater standards": men at very hard muscular work, 5,500 calories; men at moderately active muscular work, 3,400 calories; men at light to moderate muscular work, 3,050 calories; men at sedentary, or women at moderately active work, 2,700 calories.

In the last ten or fifteen years there has arisen a new school of dietetic experts, headed by Professors Chittenden and Fisher of Yale University. Professor Chittenden has published an elaborate book, "The Nutrition of Man," in which he tells of long-continued experiment upon a squad of soldiers and a group of athletes at Yale University, also upon average students and professors. He has proved conclusively that all these various groups have been able to maintain full body weight and full working efficiency upon less than half the quantity of protein food hitherto specified, and upon anywhere from one-half to two-thirds the calory value set forth in the former standards.

When I first read this book, I set to work to try its theories upon myself. During the five or six months that I lived on raw food, I took the trouble to weigh everything that I ate, and to keep a record. It is, of course, very easy to weigh raw foods exactly, and I found that I lived an active life and kept physical health upon slightly less than 2,500 calories a day. I have set this as my standard, and have accustomed myself to follow it instinctively, and without wasting any thought upon it. Sometimes I fall from grace; for I still crave the delightful cakes and candies and ice cream upon which I was brought up. I always pay the penalty, and know that I will not get back to my former state of health until I skip a meal or two, and give my system a chance to clean house. The average man will find the regimen set forth in this book austere and awe-inspiring; I do not wish to pose as a paragon of virtue, so perhaps I should quote a sarcastic girl cousin, who remarked when I was a boy that the way to my heart was with a bag of ginger-snaps. I live in the presence of candy stores and never think of their existence, but if someone brings candy into the house and puts it in front of me, I have to waste a lot of moral energy in letting it alone. A few years ago I had a young man as secretary who discovered this failing of mine, and used to afford himself immense glee by buying a box of chocolates and leaving it on top of my desk. I would give him back the box—with some of the chocolates missing—but he would persist in "forgetting it" on my desk; he would hide and laugh hilariously behind the door, until my wife discovered his nefarious doings, and warned me of them.

Professor Chittenden states quite simply the common sense procedure in the matter of food quantity. Find out by practical experiment what is the very least food upon which you can do your work without losing weight. That is the correct quantity for you, and if you are eating more, you certainly cannot be doing your body any good, and all the evidence indicates that you are doing it harm. You need not have the least fear in making this experiment that you will starve yourself. Later on, in a chapter on fasting, I shall prove to you that you carry around with you in your body sufficient reserve of food to keep you alive for eighty or ninety days; and if you draw on a small quantity of this you do not do yourself the slightest harm. Cut down the amount of your food; eat the bulky foods, which contain less calory value, and weigh yourself every day, and you will be surprised to discover how much less you need to eat than you have been accustomed to.

One of the things you will find out is that your stomach is easily fooled; it is largely guided by bulk. If you eat a meal consisting of a moderate quantity of lean meat, a very little bread, a heaping dish of turnip greens, and a big slice of watermelon, you will feel fully satisfied, yet you will not have taken in one-third the calory value that you would at an ordinary meal with gravies and dressings and dessert. The bulky kind of food is that for which your system was adapted in the days when it was shaped by nature. You have a large stomach, many times as large as you would have had if you had lived on refined and concentrated foods such as butter, sugar, olive oil, cheese and eggs. You have a long intestinal tract, adapted to slowly digesting foods, and to the work of extracting nutrition from a mass of roughage. You have a very large lower bowel, which Metchnikoff, the Russian scientist, one of the greatest minds who ever examined the problems of health, declares a survival, the relic of a previous stage of evolution, and a source of much disease. The best thing you can do with that lower bowel is to give it lots of hay, as it requires; in other words, to eat the salads and greens which contain cellulose material. This contains no food value, and does not ferment, but fills the lower bowel and stimulates it to activity.

If you eat too much food, three things may happen. First, it may not be digested, and in that case it will fill your system with poisons. Second, it may be assimilated, but not burned up by the body. In that case it has to be thrown out by the kidneys or the sweat glands, and this puts upon these organs an extra strain, to which in the long run they may be unequal. Or third, the surplus material may be stored up as fat. This is an old-time trick which nature invented to tide you over the times when food was scarce. If you were a bear, you would naturally want to eat all you could, and be as fat as possible in November, so that you might be able to hunt your prey when you came out from your winter's sleep in April. But you are not a bear, and you expect to eat your regular meals all winter; you have established a system of civilization which makes you certain of your food, and the place where you keep your surplus is in the bank, or sewed up in the mattress, or hidden in your stocking. In other words, a civilized man saves money, and the habit of storing globules of grease in the cells of his body is a survival of an old instinct, and a needless strain upon his health. Not merely does the fat man have to carry all the extra weight around with him, but his body has to keep it and tend it; and what are the effects of this is fully shown by life insurance tables. People who are five or ten per cent over weight have five or ten per cent more chance of dying all the time, while people who are five or ten per cent under weight have five or ten per cent more than the average of life expectation. There is no answer to these figures, which are the result of the tabulation of many hundreds of thousands of cases. The meaning of them to the fat person is to put himself on a diet of lean meat, green vegetables and fresh fruits, until he has brought himself down, not merely to the normal fatness of the civilized man, but to the normal leanness of the athlete, the soldier on campaign, and the student who has more important things to think about than stuffing his stomach.

There is, of course, a certain kind of leanness which is the result of ill health. There are wasting diseases; tuberculosis, for example, and anemia. There are people who worry themselves thin, and there are a few rare "spiritual" people, so-called, who fade away from lack of sufficient interest in their bodies. That is not the kind of leanness that I mean, but the active, wiry leanness, which sometimes lives a hundred years. Nearly always you will find that such people are spare eaters; and you will find that our ideal of rosy plumpness, both for adults and children, is a wholly false notion. We once had in our home as servant an Irish girl, who was what is popularly called "a picture of health," with those beautiful flaming cheeks that Irish and English women so often have. She was in her early twenties, and nobody who knew her had any idea but that her health was perfect. But one morning she was discovered in bed with one side paralyzed, and in a couple of weeks she was dead with erysipelas. The color in her cheeks had been nothing but diseased blood vessels, overloaded with food material; and with the blood in that condition, one of the tiny vessels in the brain had become clogged.

In the same way I have seen children, two or three years old, plump and rosy, and considered to be everything that children should be; but pneumonia would hit them, and in two or three days they would be at death's door. I do not mean that children should be kept hungry; on the contrary, they should have four or five meals a day, so that they do not have a chance to become too hungry. But at those meals they should eat in great part the bulky foods, which contain the natural salts needed for building the body. If a child asks for food, you may give it an apple, or you may give it a slice of bread and butter with sugar on it. The child will be equally well content in either case; but it is for you, with your knowledge of food values, to realize that the bread with butter and sugar contains two or three times as much nutriment as the apple, but contains practically none of the precious organic salts which will make the child's bones and teeth.

So far I have discussed this subject as if all foods grew on bushes outside your kitchen door, and all you had to do was to go and pick off what you wanted. But as a matter of fact, foods cost money, and under our present system of wage slavery, the amount of money the average person can spend for food is strictly limited. In a later book I am going to discuss the problem of poverty, its causes and remedies. All that I can do here is to tell you what foods you ought to have, and if society does not pay you enough for your work to enable you to buy such foods, you may know that society, is starving you, and you may get busy to demand your rights as human beings. Meantime, however, such money as you do have, you want to spend wisely, and the vast majority of you spend it very unwisely indeed.

In the first place, a great many of the simplest and most wholesome foods are cheap—often because people do not know enough to value them. We insist upon having the choice cuts of meats, because they are more tender to the teeth, but the cheaper cuts are exactly as nutritious. We insist upon having our meats loaded with fat, although fatness is an abnormal condition in an animal, and excess of fat is a grave error in diet. I live in a country where jack rabbits are a pest, and in the market they sell for perhaps one-fourth the cost of beef, and yet I can hardly ever get them, because people value them so little as food; they prefer the meat of a hog which has been wallowing in a filthy pen, and has been deliberately made so fat that it could hardly walk!

I have already spoken of prunes, a much despised and invaluable food. All the dried fruits are rich in food values, and if we could get them untreated by chemicals, they would be worth their cost. I was brought up to despise the cheaper vegetables, such as cabbage and turnips; I never tasted boiled cabbage until I was forty, and then to my great surprise I made the discovery that it is good. Raw cabbage is as valuable as any other salad; it is a trifle harder to digest for some people, but I do not believe in pampering the stomach. Both potatoes and rice are cheap and wholesome, if only we would get unpolished rice, and if we would leave the skins on the potatoes until after they are cooked. Nearly all the mineral salts of the potato are just under the outer skin, and are removed by the foolish habit of peeling them.

The prices of food differ so widely at different seasons and in different parts of the world, that there is not much profit in trying to figure how cheaply a person can live. I have found that I spend for the diet I have indicated here, from sixty to eighty cents a day. I do not buy any fancy foods, but on the other hand, I do not especially try to economize; I buy what I want of the simple everyday foods in their season. Most everyone will find that it is a good business proposition to buy the foods which he needs to keep in health. If the average workingman would add up the money he spends, not merely in the restaurants, but in the candy stores, the drug stores, the tobacco stores, and the offices of doctors and dentists, he would find, I think, that he could afford to buy himself the necessary quantity of wholesome natural foods. For a family of three, in the place where I live, enough of these foods can be purchased for a dollar a day, and this is about one-fourth what common labor is being paid, and one-eighth of what skilled labor is being paid. I will specify the foods: a pound and a half of shoulder steak, a loaf of whole wheat bread or a box of shredded wheat biscuit, a head of cabbage, a pound of prunes, and four or five pounds of apples.

There are many ways of saving in the purchase of food if you put your mind upon it. If you are buying prunes, you may pay as high as fifty cents or a dollar a pound for the big ones, and they are not a bit better than the tiny ones, which you can buy for as low as eight cents a pound in bulk. When bread is stale, the bakers sell it for half price, despite the fact that only then has it become fit to eat. If you buy canned peaches, you will pay a fancy price for them, and they will be heavy with cane sugar; but if you inquire, you find what are known as "pie peaches," put up in gallon tins without sugar, and at about half the price. The butcher will sell you what he calls "hamburg steak" at a very low price, and if you let him prepare it out of your sight, he will fill it with fat and gristle; but let him make some while you watch, and then you have a very good food. One of my diet rules is that I do not trust the capitalist system to fix me up any kind of mixed or ground or prepared foods. I have not eaten sausage since I saw it made in Chicago.

Also there is something to know about the cooking of foods, since it is possible to take perfectly good foods and spoil them by bad cooking. Once upon a time our family discovered a fireless cooker, and thought that was a wonderful invention for an absent-minded author and a wife who is given to revising manuscripts. But recent investigations which have been made into the nature of the "vitamines," food ferments which are only partly understood, suggest that prolonged cooking of food may be a great mistake. The starch has to be cooked in order to break the cell walls by the expansion of the material inside. Twenty minutes will be enough in the case of everything except beans, which need to be cooked four or five hours. Meat should be eaten rare, except in the case of pork, which harbors a parasite dangerous to the human body; therefore pork should always be thoroughly cooked. The white of eggs is made less digestible by boiling hard or frying. Eggs should never be allowed to boil; put them on in cold water, and take them off as soon as the water begins to boil. It is not necessary to cook either fresh fruit or dried. The dried fruits may be soaked and eaten raw, but I find that several fruits, especially apples and pears, do not agree with me well if they are eaten raw, so I stew them for fifteen or twenty minutes. I have no objection to canned fruits and vegetables, provided one takes the trouble in opening them to make sure there is no sign of spoiling. If you put up your own fruits, do not put in any sugar. All you have to do is to let them boil for a few minutes, and to seal them tightly while they are boiling hot. The whole secret of preserving is to exclude the air with its bacteria.

If you live on a farm, you will have no trouble in following the diet here outlined, for you can produce for yourselves all the foods that I have recommended; only do not make the mistake of shipping out your best foods, and taking back the products of a factory, just because you have read lying advertisements about them. Take your own wheat and oats and corn to the mill, and have it ground whole, and make your own breads and cereals. Try the experiment of mixing whole corn meal with water and a little salt, and baking it into hard, crisp "corn dodgers." I do not eat these—but only because I cannot buy them, and have no time to make them.

Another common article of food which I do not recommend is salted and smoked meats. I do not pretend to know the effects of large quantities of salt and saltpetre and wood smoke upon the human system, but I know that Dr. Wiley's "poison squad" proved definitely that a number of these inorganic minerals are injurious to health, and I prefer to take fresh meat when I can get it. I use a moderate quantity of common salt on meat and potatoes, because there seems to be a natural craving for this. I know that many health enthusiasts insist that I am thus putting a strain on my kidneys, but I will wait until these health enthusiasts make clear to me why deer and cattle and horses in a wild state will travel many miles to a salt-lick. I have learned that it is easy to make plausible statements about health, but not so easy to prove them. For example, I was told that it is injurious to drink water at meals, and for years I religiously avoided the habit; but it occurred to some college professor to find out if this was really true, and he carried on a series of experiments which proved that the stomach works better when its contents are diluted. The only point about drinking at meals is that you should not use the liquid to wash down your food without chewing it.

I can suggest two other ways by which you may save money on food. One is by not eating too much, and another is by eating all that you buy. The amount of food that is wasted by the people of America would feed the people of any European nation. The amount of food that is thrown out from any one of our big American leisure class hotels would feed the children of a European town. I think it may fairly be described as a crime to throw into the garbage pail food which might nourish human life. In our family we have no garbage pail. What little waste there is, we burn in the stove, and my wife turns it into roses. It consists of the fat which we cannot help getting at the butcher's, and the bones of meat, and the skins of some fruits and vegetables. It would never enter into our minds to throw out a particle of bread, or meat, or other wholesome food. If we have something that we fear may spoil, we do not throw it out, but put it into a saucepan and cook it for a few minutes. If you will make the same rule in your home, you will stop at least that much of the waste of American life; and as to the big leisure class hotels, and the banquet tables of the rich—just wait a few years, and I think the social revolution will attend to them!

CHAPTER XXII

FOODS AND POISONS

(Concludes the subject of diet, and discusses the effect upon the system of stimulants and narcotics.)

A few years ago there died an old gentleman who had devoted some twenty years of his life to teaching people to chew their food. Horace Fletcher was his name, and his ideas became a fad, and some people carried them to comical extremes. But Fletcher made a real discovery; what he called "the food filter." This is the automatic action of the swallowing apparatus, whereby nature selects the food which has been sufficiently prepared for digestion. If you chew a mouthful of food without ever performing the act of swallowing, you will find that the food gradually disappears. What happens is that all of it which has been reduced to a thin paste will slip unnoticed down your throat, and you may go on putting more food into your mouth, and chewing, and can eat a whole meal without ever performing the act of swallowing. Fletcher claimed that this is the proper way to eat, and that you can train yourself to follow this method. I have tried his idea and adopted it. One of my diet rules, to which there is no exception, is that if I haven't the time to chew my food properly, I haven't the time to eat; I skip that meal.

The habit of bolting food is a source of disease. To be sure, the carnivorous animals bolt their food, but they are tougher than we are, and do not carry the burden of a large brain and a complex nervous system. If you swallow your meals half chewed, and wash them down with liquids, you may get away with it for a while, but some day you will pay for it with dyspepsia and nervous troubles. And the same thing applies to your habit of jumping up from meals and rushing away to work, whether it be work of the muscles, or of brain and nerves. Proper digestion requires the presence of a quantity of blood in the walls of the stomach and digestive tract. It requires the attention of your subconscious mind, and this means rest of muscles and brain centers. If you cannot rest for an hour after meals, omit that meal, or make it a light one, of fruit juices, which are almost immediately absorbed by the stomach, and of salads, which do not ferment. You may rest assured that it will not hurt you to skip a meal, and make up for it when you have time to be quiet. I have been many times in my life under very intense and long continued nervous strain; for example, during the Colorado coal strike, I led a public demonstration which kept me in a state of excitement all the day and a good part of the night several weeks. During this period I ate almost nothing; a baked apple and a cup of custard would be as near as I would go to a meal, and as a result I came through the experience without any injury whatever to my health. I lost perhaps ten pounds in weight, but that was quickly made up when I settled back to a normal way of life.

I have been on camping trips when I had a great deal of hard work to do, carrying a canoe long distances on my back, or paddling it forty miles a day. On the mornings of such a trip I have seen a guide cook himself an elaborate breakfast of freshly baked bread, bacon, and even beans, and make a hearty meal and then go straight to work. My meal, on the contrary, would consist of a small dish of stewed prunes, or perhaps some huckleberries or raspberries, if they could be found. I will not say that I could do as much as the guide, because he was used to it, and I was not. But I can say this—if I had eaten his breakfast at the start of the day, I would have been dead before night; and I mean the word "dead" quite literally. I know a man who started to climb Whiteface mountain in the Adirondacks. He climbed half way, and then ate lunch, which consisted of nine hard boiled eggs. Then he started to climb the rest of the mountain, and dropped dead of acute indigestion.

There are few poisons which can affect the system more quickly, or more dangerously, than a mass of food which is not digested. The stomach is an ideal forcing-house for the breeding of bacteria. It provides warmth and moisture, and you, in your meal, provide the bacteria and the material upon which they thrive. Under normal conditions, the stomach pours out a gastric juice which kills the bacteria; but let this gastric juice for any reason be lacking—because your nervous energy has gone somewhere else, or because your blood-stream, from which the gastric juice must be made, has been drawn away to the muscles by hard labor; then you have a yeast-pot, with great quantities of gases and poisons. In acute cases the results are evident enough: violent pains and convulsions, followed by coma and the turning black of the body. But what you should understand is that you may produce a milder case of such poisoning, and may do it day after day habitually, and little by little your vital organs will be weakened by the strain.

It does not make any difference at what hour of the twenty-four you take the great bulk of your food. It is one of the commonest delusions that you get some strengthening effect from your food immediately, and must have this strength in order to do hard work. To be sure, there are substances, such as grape-sugar, which require practically no digesting; you can hold them in the mouth, and they will be digested by the saliva, and absorbed at once into the blood-stream. But unless you have been starved for a long period you do not need to get your strength in this rush fashion. If you ate your normal meals on the previous day, your blood-stream is fully supplied with nutriment which has been put through a long process of preparation, and you can get up in the morning and work all day, if necessary, upon what is already in your system. To be sure, you may feel hungry, and even faint, but that is merely a matter of habit; your system is accustomed to taking food and expects it. But if you are a laborer doing hard work, you can easily train yourself to eat a light meal in the morning, and another light meal at noon, and to eat a hearty meal when your work is done and you can rest. Two light meals and a hearty meal are all that any system needs, and you can prove it to yourself by trying it, and watching your weight once a week.

I have tried many experiments, and the conclusion to which I have come is that there is no virtue in any particular meal-hours or any particular number of meals. For several years I tried the experiment of two meals a day. I was living a retired life, and had little contact with the world, and I would make a hearty meal at ten o'clock in the morning, and another at five in the afternoon. But later on I found that inconvenient, and now I take a light breakfast, and two moderate-sized meals at the conventional hours of lunch and dinner. I can arrange my own time, so after meal times is when I get my reading done. Sometimes, when I am tired, I feel sleepy after meals, but I have learned not to yield to this impulse. I do not know how to explain this; I have observed that animals sleep after eating, and it appears to be a natural thing to do; but I know that if I go to sleep after a meal, nature makes clear to me that I have made a mistake, and I do not repeat it. I never eat at night, and always go to bed on an empty stomach, so I am always hungry when I open my eyes in the morning. I never know what it is not to be hungry at meal times, and my habits are so regular that I could set my watch by my stomach.

Another common habit which is harmful is eating between meals. I have known people who are accustomed to nibble at food nearly all the time. Shelley records that he tried it as an experiment, thinking it might be a convenient way to get digestion done—but he found that it did not work. The stomach is apparently meant to work in pulses; to do a job of digesting, and then to rest and accumulate the juices for another job. It will accustom itself to a certain régime, and will work accordingly, but if, when it has half digested a load of food, you pile more food in on top, you make as much trouble as you would make in your kitchen if you required your cook to prepare another meal before she has cleaned up after the last one. Three times a day is enough for any adult to eat. Children require to eat oftener, because their bodies are more active, and they not merely have to keep up weight, but to add to it. The simplest way to arrange matters with children is to give them three good meals at the hours when adults eat, and then to give them a couple of pieces of fruit between breakfast and lunch, and again between lunch and supper. I have never seen a child who would not be satisfied with this, when once the habit was established.

I have already spoken of the cooking and serving of food. I consider that the "gastronomic art," as it is pompously called, is ninety-nine per cent plain rubbish. To be sure, if foods are appetizingly prepared, and look good and smell good and taste good, they will cause the gastric juices to flow abundantly, as the Russian scientist Pavlov has demonstrated by practical experiment with the stomach-pump. But I know without any stomach-pump that the best thing to make my gastric juices flow is hard work and a spare diet. When I come home from five sets of tennis, and have a cold shower and a rub-down, my gastric juices will flow for a piece of cold beefsteak and a cold sweet potato, quite as well as for anything that is served by a leisure class "chef." Needless to say, I want food to be fresh, and I want it to be clean, but I have other things to do with my time and money than to pamper my appetites and encourage food whims.

If you have a grandmother, or ever had one, you know what grandmothers tell you about "hot nourishing food"; but I have tried the experiment, and satisfied myself that there is absolutely no difference in nourishing qualities between hot food and cold food. If you chew your food sufficiently, it will all be ninety-eight and six-tenths degree food when it gets to your stomach, and that is the way your stomach wants it. Of course, if you have been out in a blizzard, and are chilled, and want to restore the body temperature, a hot drink will be one of the quickest ways, and if the emergency is extreme, you may even add a stimulant. On the other hand, if you are suffering from heat, it is sensible to cool your body by a cold drink. But you should use as much judgment with yourself as you would with a horse, which you do not permit to drink a lot of cold water when he is heated up, and is going into his stall to stand still.

I have mentioned the word "stimulants," and this opens a large subject. There are drugs which affect the body in two different ways: some excite the nerves, and through the nerves the heart and blood-stream, to more intense activity; others have the effect of deadening the nerves, and dulling the sense of exhaustion and pain. One of these groups is called stimulants, and the other is called narcotics; but as a matter of fact the stimulants are really narcotics, because they operate by dulling the nerves whose function it is to prevent the over-accumulation of fatigue poisons; in other words, they keep the nerves and muscles from knowing that they are tired, and so they go on working.

It is possible, of course, to conceive of an emergency in which that is necessary. Once upon a time, on a hunting trip, I had been traveling all day, and was caught in a rain storm, and exhausted and chilled to the bone; I had to make camp without a fire, so when I got the tent up I wrapped myself in blankets and drank a couple of tablespoons full of whiskey. That is the only time I have ever taken whiskey in my life, and it warmed me almost instantly, and did me no harm. In the same way there were two or three occasions when I was on the verge of a nervous breakdown, and could not sleep, and let the doctor give me a sleeping powder. But in each case I knew that I was fooling with a dangerous habit, and I did no more fooling than necessary. No one should make use of either stimulants or narcotics except in extreme emergency, and never but a few times in a lifetime. What you should do is to change your habits so that you will not need to over-strain.

All these drugs are habit forming; that is to say, they leave the body no better, and with a craving for a repetition of the relief. When you are tired, it is because your muscles and nerves are storing up fatigue poisons more rapidly than your blood-stream can get rid of them. You need to know about this condition, and exhaustion and pain are nature's protective warning. If you put a stop to the warning, you are as unintelligent as the Eastern despots who used to cut off the head of the messenger who brought bad tidings. If, when you have a headache, you go into a drug store and let the druggist mix you one of those white fizzy drinks, what you are doing is not to get rid of the poisons in your blood-stream, but merely to reduce the action of your heart, so as to keep the blood from pressing so fast into the aching blood vessels and nerves. You may try that trick with your heart a number of times, but sooner or later you will try it once too often—your heart will stop a little bit quicker than you meant it to!

Drugs are poisons, and their action depends upon their poisoning some particular portion of the body, and temporarily paralyzing it. And bear this in mind, they are none the less poisonous because they are "natural" products. You can kill yourself by cyanide of potassium, which comes out of a chemist's retort; but you can kill yourself just as dead with laudanum, which comes out of a plant, or with the contents of the venom sac of a snake. You are poisoning yourself none the less certainly if you use alcohol, which is made from the juices of beautiful fruits, and has had hosts of famous poets writing songs about it; or you can poison yourself with the caffein which you get in a lovely brown bean which comes from Brazil, fragrant to the nostrils and delicious to the taste. You may drink wine and tea and coffee for a hundred years, and have your picture published in the newspapers as a proof that these habits conduce to health; but nothing will be said about the large number of people who practiced these habits, and didn't live so long, and about how long they might have lived if they hadn't practiced these habits.

I was brought up in the South, and my "elders" belonged to a generation which had grown up in war time. For this reason many of the men both drank and smoked to excess, and in my boyhood I lived among them and watched them, and with the help of advice from a wise mother, I conceived a horror of every kind of stimulant. The alcoholic poets could not fool me; I had been in the alcoholic wards of the hospitals. I had seen one man after another, beautiful and kindly and gracious men, dragged down into a pit of torment and shame.

Alcohol is, I think, the greatest trap that nature ever set for the feet of the human race. It is responsible for more degradation and misery than any other evil in the world; and I say this, knowing well that my Socialist friends will cry, "What about Capitalism?" My answer is that I doubt if there ever would have been any Capitalism in the world, if it had not been for alcohol. If the workers had not been systematically poisoned, and all their savings taken from them by the gin-mill, they would never have submitted to the capitalist system, they would have built the co-operative commonwealth at the time they were building the first factories. I listen to the arguments of my radical friends about "personal liberty," but I note that in Russia, when it was a question of making a practical revolution and keeping it alive, the first thing the leaders did was to drag out the contents of the wine-cellars of the palaces, and smash them in the gutters.

Tea and coffee are, of course, much milder in their effects than alcohol; you can play with them longer, and the punishment will be less severe. But if you make habitual use of them, you will pay the penalty which all drugs exact from the system. Your brain and your nerve centers will be less sensitive, less capable of working except under the influence of drugs; their reacting power will be dulled, and they will wear out more quickly. I have watched the slaves of the "morning cup of coffee," and know how they suffer when they do not get it. Likewise, I have watched the tea drinkers. It is comical to live in England, and see all the able-bodied men obliged to leave their work at four o'clock in the afternoon, and seek the regular stimulus for their tired nerves. If you are to meet anybody, it is always for "tea" that the ceremony is set, and if you refuse to drink tea, your hostess will be uncomfortable, unable to talk about anything but the strange, incredible notion that one can live without tea. I discovered after a while the solution of this problem; I would say that I preferred a little hot water, if you please, and so my hostess would pour me a cup of hot water, and I would sit and gravely sip it, and everybody would be perfectly content: I was conforming to the outward appearance of normality, which is what the British conventions require.

I have never drunk a cup of coffee, so I do not know what its effect on me would be. But some fifteen years ago I drank a glass of very weak iced tea at eight o'clock in the evening, and did not get to sleep until four or five the next morning. So I know that there is really a drug in tea. I know also that I might accustom my system to it, just as I might learn to poison my lungs with nicotine without being made immediately and suddenly ill; but why should I wish to do this? Life is so interesting to me that I do not need to stimulate my brain centers in order to appreciate the thrill of it. And when I am tired, I can rest myself by listening to music, or by reading a worthwhile novel—things which I have found do not leave the after effects of nicotine.

I remember the first time I met Jack London. Our meeting consisted in good part of his "kidding" me, because I was lacking in the congenial vices of the café. He told me how much I had missed, because I had never been drunk; One ought to try the great adventure, at least once! Poor Jack is gone, because his kidneys gave out at forty; and nothing could seem more ungracious than to point out that I am still alive, and finding life enjoyable. Yet, in this book we are trying to find out how to live, and if there are habits which wreck and destroy a magnificent physique, and bring a great genius to death at the age of forty—surely the rest of us want to know about it, and to be warned in time. I mention Jack London in this connection, because he has said the last word on the subject of alcohol. Read "John Barleycorn," and especially read between the lines of it, and you will not need my argument to persuade you to be glad that the Eighteenth Amendment has been written into the Constitution, and that it is your duty as a Socialist, not merely to obey it, but to vote for its enforcement.

I am proceeding on the assumption that your life is of importance to you; that you have a job to do which you know to be worth while, and to which you desire to apply your powers. You agree with me that the workers of the world are suffering, and that it is necessary for them to find their freedom, and that this takes hard work and hard thinking. You may say that I exaggerate the amount of harm that is done to the system by tea and coffee, alcohol and tobacco. Well, let us assume that in moderate quantities they do no harm at all: even so, I have the right to ask you to show that they do some good; otherwise, surely, it is a mistake for the workers to spend their savings upon them.

Consider, for example, the amount of money which the wage slaves of the world spend upon tobacco. Suppose they could be persuaded for two or three years to spend this amount upon good reading matter—do you not think there would be an improvement in their condition? Surely you cannot maintain that the use of tobacco is necessary to the activities of the brain! Surely you do not think that a man has to have a cigarette in order to stimulate his thoughts, or to smoke a pipe to rest himself after his work is done! I offer myself as evidence in such a controversy; I have written as many books as any man in the radical movement, and the sum total of my lifetime smoking amounts to one-half of one cigarette. I tried that when I was eight years old, and somebody told me a policeman would arrest me if he caught me, and I threw away the cigarette, and ran and hid in an alley, and have not yet got over my scare.

In the "Journal for Industrial Hygiene" for October, 1920, is an article entitled "Fatigue and Efficiency of Smokers in a Strenuous Mental Occupation." Experiments were conducted among telegraph operators, and the result showed that "the heavy smokers of the group show a higher output rate at the beginning of the day than the light smokers, but their rate falls off more markedly in the late hours, and their production for the whole day is definitely less than that of the light smokers. The heavy smokers also show less ability than the light smokers to respond to increasing pressure of work in the late hours of the day by handling their full share of the work presented."

One point upon which every medical authority agrees is—that the use of nicotine is of deadly effect upon the immature organism. Half-grown youths who smoke cigarettes will never be full-sized men; they will never have normal lungs or a normal heart. And likewise, all authorities agree about the effect of smoking upon the organism of women. I gave what little help I could to the task of helping to set women free, and to make them the equals of men; but I was always pained when I discovered that some of my feminist friends understood by woman's emancipation no more than her right to adopt men's vices. I would say to these ardent young female radicals, who cultivate the art of dangling a cigarette from their lower lip, and sip cocktails out of coffee-cups in Greenwich Village cafés, that they will never be able to bear sound children; but I know that this would not interest them—they don't want to bear any children at all. So I say that they will never be able to think straight thoughts, and will be nervous invalids when they are thirty.

We went to war to make the world safe for democracy, and we put several millions of our young men into armies, and if there were any of them who did not already know how to smoke cigarettes, they learned it under official sanction. So now we have a national tobacco bill that runs up to two billions, and will insure us a new generation of "Class C" rating. Speaking to the young radicals who are reading my books, I say: We want to make the world over, to make it a place of freedom and kindness, instead of the hell of greed and hate that it is today. For that purpose we need a new moral code, and we can never win our victory without it. I have attended radical conventions, sitting in unventilated halls amid clouds of tobacco smoke, and listening to men wrangle all through the day and a great part of the night; I have watched the fatal dissensions in the movement, the quarrelings of the right wingers and the left wingers and all stages and degrees in between, and I have wondered—not jestingly, but in pitying earnest—how much of all those personalities and factional misunderstanding had their origin in carbon dioxide and nicotine. There is no use suggesting such ideas to the older men, whose habits are fixed; but a new generation is coming on, with a new vision of the enormous task before it; and is it too much to expect of these young men and women, that they shall realize in advance the grim tasks they have to do, and shall learn to run the machine of their body so as to get out of it the maximum amount of service? Is it too much to hope for, that some day we shall have a race of young fighters for truth and justice, who are willing to live abstemious lives, and consecrate themselves to the task of delivering mankind from wage slavery and war?

CHAPTER XXIII

MORE ABOUT HEALTH

(Discusses the subjects of breathing and ventilation, clothing, bathing and sleep.)

In discussing the question of health, we have given the greater part of the space to the subject of diet, for the reason that experience has convinced us that diet is two-thirds of health, and that nearly always in disease you find errors of diet playing a part. There are, however, other important factors of health, now to be discussed.

Everything of which the body makes use is taken in the form of food and drink, with the exception of one substance, the oxygen we get out of the air. Every time we draw a breath we take in a certain amount of oxygen, and every time we expel a breath, we drive out a certain amount of a gas called carbon dioxide, which is what the body makes of the fuel it burns. The body can get along for several days without water, and for two or three months without food, but it can only get along for two or three minutes without oxygen. It should be obvious that when the body expels carbon dioxide, with a slight mixture of other more poisonous gases, and sucks back what it expects will be a fresh supply of oxygen, it wants to get oxygen, and not the same gases it has just expelled, nor gases which have been expelled from the lungs of other people.

In the days when primitive man lived outdoors, he did not have to think about this problem. When he breathed poison from his lungs, the moving air of nature blew it away, and the infinite vegetation of nature took the carbon dioxide and turned it back into oxygen. And even when man built himself shelters, he was not cunning enough to make them air-tight; he had to leave a big hole for the smoke to get out, and smaller holes through which to get light. But now our wonderful civilization has solved these problems; we make our walls of air-tight plaster, and we have invented a substance which will admit light without admitting air. So we have the "white plague" of tuberculosis, and so we have innumerable minor plagues of coughs and colds and sore throats.

In the summer time the solution of the problem is easy. Have as many doors and windows in your home as possible, and keep them open, and have nothing in your home to make dust or to retain dust. But then comes stormy and cold weather, and you have to close your doors and windows, and keep your home at a higher temperature than the air outside. How shall you do this, and at the same time get a continual supply of fresh air?

I will take the various methods of heating one by one. The problem in each case is simple and can be made clear in a sentence or two.

First, the open fireplace. This is a perfect solution, if you have enough fuel, and do not have to worry about the waste of heat. An open fireplace draws out all the air in the room in a short time, and you do not have to bother about opening doors or windows; you may be sure that the air is getting in through some cracks, or else the fire would not burn.

Second, a wood or coal or gas stove in the room, provided with a proper vent, so that all the gases of combustion are drawn up the chimney. This changes the air more slowly than an open fireplace, but it does the work fairly well. All that you have to be careful about is that your vent is sufficiently large and is working properly. If your fire does not "draw," you will have smoke or coal-gas in the house, and this is bad for the lungs; but worse for the lungs is a gas that you can neither see nor smell nor taste, the deadly carbon monoxide. This gas is produced by incomplete combustion, and whenever you see yellow flames from gas or coal, you are apt to have this poisonous substance. Small quantities of it are sufficient to cause violent headaches, and repeated doses of it are fatal. Men who work in garages which are not properly ventilated run this risk all the time, because carbon monoxide is one of the products of imperfect combustion in the gas engine.

Next, the furnace. A furnace sends fresh warm air into your house; the only trouble is that it takes out all the moisture, and some authorities say that this is bad for the lungs and throat. I do not know whether this is true, but all furnaces are supposed to have a water chamber to supply moisture to the air, and you should keep a pan of water on every stove or radiator in your house.

Next, steam heat, which includes hot-water heating. This is one of the abominations of our civilization, and one of the methods by which our race is committing suicide. There is nothing wrong about steam heat in itself; the room is warmed in a harmless way; but the trouble is it stays warm only so long as the doors and windows are kept shut. You are in an air-tight box, and can be warm provided you do not mind being suffocated. The moment you open a door or window, you have a cold draft on your feet, and if you wish to change the air entirely you have to let out all the heat; so, of course, you never do change it entirely, but go on breathing the same air over and over, and every time you breathe it the condition of your body is a little more reduced.

The solution of this problem is not to heat the air in the room, but to use your steam coils to heat fresh air, and then drive this air, already warmed, into the room, at the same time providing a vent through which the old air can be pushed out. This is the hot air system of heating, and it requires some kind of engine or dynamo, and therefore is expensive. It has been installed in a few office buildings and theaters. One of the most perfect systems I ever inspected is in the building of the New York Stock Exchange, where the air is warmed in winter, and cooled in summer, and freed from dust, and exactly the right quantity is supplied. It is a humorous commentary upon our civilization that we take perfect care of the breathing apparatus of our stock-gamblers, but pay no attention to the breathing apparatus of our senators and congressmen, whose one business in life is to use their lungs. The stately old building with its white marble domes looks impressive in moving pictures and on illustrated postcards, but it has no system of ventilation whatever, and is a death-trap to the poor wretches who are compelled to spend their days, and sometimes their nights, within its walls. This contrast is one symptom of the rise of industrial capitalism and the collapse of political democracy.

We have reserved to the last a method of heating which is the worst, and can only be described as a crime against health: the use of gas and oil stoves set out in the middle of the room, without a vent, and discharging their fumes into the room. These stoves are simply instruments of slow death, and their manufacture should be prohibited by law. In the meantime, what you have to do is to refuse to live in a room or to work in an office where such stoves are used. I have heard dealers insist that this or the other kind of gas or oil stove was so contrived as to consume all the fumes. Do not let anybody fool you with such nonsense. There has never been any form of combustion devised which consumes all the fumes. No such thing can be, because the products of combustion are not combustible. The so-called "wickless blue flame" stoves do burn all the oil, and a properly regulated gas stove will burn all the gas, but that simply means that it turns the oil and gas into carbon dioxide, the very substance which your lungs are working day and night to get out of your body.

Moreover, there is no oil or gas stove which ever burns perfectly all the time, either because there is too much gas or insufficient air. Oil and gas stoves sometimes give a partly yellow flame. You can cause them to give a yellow flame at any time by blowing air against them, and that yellow flame means imperfect combustion, and a probability of the deadly carbon monoxide. These facts are known to every chemist and to every student of hygiene, and the fact that civilized people continue to burn such oil and gas stoves in their homes and offices is simply one more proof that our civilization values human welfare and health at nothing whatever in comparison with profits.

Not merely should you see that you have a continuous supply of fresh air in your home, but you should try to keep down dust in your home, and especially fine particles of lint. Once upon a time our ancestors were unable to make houses and floors tight, and so they put rugs on the floors and hung tapestries on the walls to keep out the wind. We civilized people are able to make both floors and walls absolutely tight, and yet we continue to use rugs and curtains, it being the first principle of our education that propriety requires us to continue to do the things which our ancestors did. I am unable to think of a more silly or stupid thing in the world than a rug or a curtain, but I have lived in the house with them all my life, because, alas, the ladies cannot be happy otherwise. They want their homes to be "pretty," and so they continue to set dust traps, and to set themselves futile jobs of house cleaning and shopping.

Not all of us are able to be out of doors as much as we ought to be, but all of us spend seven or eight hours out of every twenty-four in sleep, and this time at least we ought to spend out of doors. I understand that this is futile advice to give to the very poor. I was poor myself for many years, and had to put all my clothes on at night in order to keep warm, and even then I could not always do it. Nevertheless, from the time I first realized the importance of ventilation I never slept in a room with a closed window.

I say, sleep outdoors if you possibly can. You do not have to be afraid of exposure, for cold will not hurt you if you keep your body in proper condition. I have slept out in a rubber blanket, with the rain beating on my head and face; I have spread a rubber blanket on a hummock in the midst of a swamp, and waked up in the morning with my hair and face soaked in cold, white fog, but I never caught cold from such things; there is no harm whatever in dampness or in "night air," if you are in proper condition. Of course, you may get your ears frostbitten in the middle of winter, but you can have a sleeping hood to remove that danger.

The "nature cure" enthusiasts, who lay so much stress upon an outdoor life, also insist that the wearing of clothes is a harmful civilized custom. They urge us to take "sun baths" and to "ventilate the skin." Now, as a matter of fact, the skin does not breathe, it merely gives out moisture, and it does not give out any less because we have clothing on us, provided the clothing is dry and clean, and will absorb moisture. But bye and bye the clothing becomes loaded with the waste substances given out by the skin, and then it will absorb no more, and if you do not change your clothing, no doubt it may have some effect upon health.

But the principal evil of civilized clothing is that it binds the body and prevents the free play of the muscles, and, more important yet, stops the free circulation of the blood. I have already discussed hats, which are the principal cause of baldness. I will go to the other extremity of the body, and mention tight shoes, which, strange as it may seem, cause headaches and colds. You will be able to find a few civilized men with normal feet, but you will hardly ever find a woman whose toes are not crowded together and misshapen. I have said that the human body is one organism, and that it is fed and its health maintained by the blood-stream; I say now that the circulation of the blood is one thing, and if you block it at any one place, you block it everywhere. Of course, not all the blood-stream goes down into the feet, but some of it does, and if it is clogged in the feet, and the blood vessels cramped and crowded, there is a certain amount of poison kept in the system, which the system should have got rid of.

Why do women wear tight shoes? Because the leisure class members of their sex have been kept in harems and used as the playthings of men. To be fragile and delicate was the thing admired by the masters of wealth, and to have small hands and feet was a sign that women belonged to this parasite class. Therefore at all hazards women's feet must be kept small, even at the expense of their health and happiness; and so they put themselves up on several inches of heels, which cause them to toddle around like marionettes on a stage, with all their toes crowded down into a lump.

Why do men wear tight bands around their scalps, which cause their hair to drop out, and tight, stiff columns around their necks, which stop the circulation of the blood into their heads, and cause them to have headaches instead of ideas? The reason is that for ages the rulers of the tribe have wished to demonstrate publicly their superiority to the common herd, which does the menial tasks. In England all gentlemen wear tall black silk band-boxes on their heads, and in America they have a choice among several varieties of round tight boxes. All men who work in offices wear stiffly starched collars and cuffs, as a means of demonstrating their superiority to the common workers, who have to sweat at their necks. I think it is not too much to hope that when class exploitation is done away with, we shall also get rid of these class symbols, and choose our clothing because it is warm and comfortable, and not according to the perverted imbecilities of "style."

The skin gives out perspiration which is greasy; also the skin is constantly growing, putting out layers of cells which dry up and are worn off. We need to bathe with soap to remove the grease, and we need to rub with a towel to brush away the dead cells of the skin, so that the pores may be kept open. No one is taking care of his body who does not wash and rub it once every twenty-four hours, and once or twice a week with warm water and soap. It is often stated that hot baths are weakening, but I have never found it so; however, I think it is a bad practice to pamper the body, which should be accustomed to the shock of cold water. The rule as to bathing, both as to temperature and time, is simple. If, after the bath and rub-down, your body has reacted and you feel vigorous and fresh, that bath has done you good. If, on the other hand, you feel chilled and depressed, then you have been too long in the water, or its temperature was too low. Every person has to find his own rules in such matters. The only general rule is that as one grows older the body reacts less quickly.

All day, as we work and think, we store up more poisons in our cells than the body can get rid of, and the time comes when the cells are so loaded with poisons that we have to stop for a while, and let our blood-stream clean house. The quantity of sleep one needs is a problem like that of cold water; each person has to find his own rule. In general, one needs less and less sleep as one grows older. Infants sleep the greater part of the time; growing children should sleep ten or eleven hours, adults seven or eight, and old people, unless they have let themselves get fat, generally do not want to sleep more than six, and part of this in short naps. When you sleep, your bodily energies relax, and you make less heat, therefore you need extra clothing; but this clothing should never cover the mouth and nose, nor should it be so heavy as to make breathing a burden. If you are in good condition, it will do you no harm to be chilly when you sleep, except that you do not sleep so soundly. Sleeping too much is just as harmful as sleeping too little. Nature will tell you that. The important thing, as in all other problems of health, is to have something interesting to think about, some exciting work to do in the world, and then you will sleep as little as you have too.

CHAPTER XXIV

WORK AND PLAY

(Deals with the question of exercise, both for the idle and the overworked.)

In discussing the important question of exercise, there is one fundamental fact to begin with: that our present civilization divides men sharply into two classes, those who do not get enough exercise, and those who get too much. Obviously it would be folly to make the same recommendations to the two classes.

I begin with those who get too much exercise. They include a great number, probably the majority of those who do the manual work of the world. They include the farmers and the farm-hands, who work from dawn to sunset, and sometimes by lantern light. They include also the farmers' wives, the kitchen slaves of whom the old couplet tells:

"Man's work ends from sun to sun,

But woman's work is never done."

I am aware that men have worked that way for countless ages, and yet the race is still surviving; but I am aware also that men wither up with rheumatism, and contract chronic diseases of the kidneys and the blood vessels, consequent upon the creation of greater quantities of fatigue poisons than the body can regularly eliminate.

I have very little interest in the past, and none whatever in finding fault with it. My purpose is to criticize the present for the benefit of the future, and therefore I say that modern machinery and the whole development of modern large-scale production make it absolutely unnecessary that women should slave all their waking hours in kitchens, or that men should slave all day. I say it is monstrous folly that men should work for twelve-hour stretches in steel mills, and for ten and eleven hours in factories and mines. Organized labor has adopted the slogan, "Eight hours for work, eight hours for sleep, eight hours for play"; but my slogan is "Four hours for work, four hours for study, eight hours for sleep, and eight hours for play."

I know, and am prepared to demonstrate to any thinking man, that modern civilization can produce, not merely all the necessities, but all the comforts of life for every man, woman and child in the community, by the expenditure of four hours a day work of the adult, able-bodied men and women. So to all the wage slaves of the factories and mines, the fields and the kitchens, I say that too much exercise is what is the matter with you, and what you need is to get off in a quiet nook in the woods and read a good novel, not merely for a few hours, but for a few months, until you get over the effects of capitalist civilization. I know that not many of you can get away as yet, but I urge you to insist upon getting away, to fight for the chance to get away; and I will here suggest a few of the novels for you to read when finally you do get away. I choose the easy ones, which the dullest and most tired of you will love; I say, make up your mind to read these thirty-two books before you die, and do not let the world cheat you out of your chance!

Mark Twain: A Connecticut Yankee in King Arthur's Court. Charles D. Stewart: The Fugitive Blacksmith. W. Clark Russell: The Wreck of the Grosvenor. R. L. Stevenson: Treasure Island, Kidnapped. Jack London: The Sea Wolf, The Call of the Wild, Martin Eden. Joseph Conrad: Youth. H. G. Wells: The War of the Worlds, When the Sleeper Wakes, The Sea Lady, The History of Mr. Polly, The Food of the Gods, The Island of Dr. Moreau. Upton Sinclair: The Jungle, King Coal, Jimmie Higgins, 100 Per Cent. Theodore Dreiser: Sister Carrie. George Moore: Esther Waters. Frank Norris: The Octopus. Brand Whitlock: The Turn of the Balance. De Foe: Robinson Crusoe. Fielding: Tom Jones, Jonathan Wild the Great. Thackeray: The Adventures of Barry Lyndon. Marmaduke Pickthall: The Adventures of Hadji Baba. Blasco Ibanez: The Fruit of the Vine. Frank Harris: Montes the Matador. Frederik van Eeden: The Quest. Tolstoi: Resurrection.

And now for the people who do not get enough exercise. In the armies of King Cyrus it was the law that every man was required to sweat once every twenty-four hours, and that is still the law for every business man and office-worker and writer of books. There is no substitute for it, and there is no health without it. I have heard Dr. Kellogg say that the modern woman sends out her health with her washing, and I have heard the leisure class ladies at the Sanitarium discuss this cryptic utterance and wonder what he meant by it. I know that there is use telling leisure class ladies what exercise at the wash-tub would do for their abdomens and backs. I will only tell them that unless they can find some kind of vigorous activity which keeps them in a free perspiration for an hour or two each day, they will never be really well, and will never bear children without agony and abortion.

For myself, I have found that the minimum is three or four times a week. Unless I get that much hard exercise I am soon in trouble. So my advice to the business man is to take off his coat and collar and turn out and help his truck-man; my advice to the white collar slave is to get a part-time job, and dig ditches the rest of the time. To the man who has cares which pursue him, and likewise to the ardent student and brain-worker, I say that they should find, not merely exercise, but play. The distinction between the two things is important. There can be play that is not exercise, for example cards and chess; and, of course, there can be exercise that is not play. What you must have is something that is both play and exercise; something that not merely causes your heart to beat fast, and your lungs to pump fast, and your sweat glands to throw out poisons from your body, but something that fully occupies your mind and gives your higher brain centers a chance to relax.

Our civilization has very largely destroyed the possibility of play and the spirit of play. We civilized people no longer know what play is, and regard the desire to play as something abnormal—a form of vice. We allow children to play after school hours, and on Saturdays; but for grown-up, serious-minded men and women to want to play would be almost as disreputable as for them to want to get drunk. What could foe more pitiful than the spectacle of tens of thousands of men crowding into our baseball parks and amusement fields to watch other men play for them! Imagine, if you can, a crowd of people gathering in a restaurant or theater to watch other people *eat* for them! Imagine yourself a man from Mars, coming down to a world with so many people in want, and finding whole classes of men forbidden to do any work, under penalty of disgrace, and compelled, in order to exercise their muscles, to pull on rubber straps and lift weights and wave dumb-bells and Indian clubs in the air—methods of expending their muscular energy which are respectable because they accomplish nothing!

When I was a boy, I was fond of all kinds of games. I was a good tennis player, and in the country an incessant hunter and fisherman. When on the city streets we boys could not find any other game to play, we would get up on the roofs of the houses and throw clothes-pins and snow-balls at the "Dagoes" working in the nearby excavations; so we had the fine game of being chased by the "Dagoes," with the chance, real or imaginary, of having a knife stuck into us. But then, as I grew older, and became aware of the pain and misery of the world, I lost my interest in games, and for ten years or so I never played; I did nothing but study and write. So my health gave way, and I had the problem of restoring it, and I spent some twenty years wrestling with this problem, before I thoroughly convinced myself on the point that there can be no such thing as sound and permanent health without a certain amount of play.

I don't think there is any kind of hard physical work I failed to try, in the course of my experiments. I rode horseback, and took long walks, and climbed mountains, and swam, and dug gardens, and chopped down whole groves of trees and cut them up and carried them to the fireplace. I have done this latter work for a whole winter in the country, several hours every day, and it has done my health no good to speak of; I have been ready for a breakdown at the end of it. The reason is that all the time I was doing these things with my body, I was going right on working my brain. While I was swimming or climbing a mountain or galloping on horseback, I was absorbed in the next chapter of the book I was writing, so that I literally did not know where I was. I would make up my mind that I would not think about my work, and would make desperate efforts not to do so; but it was like walking along the edge of a slippery ditch—sooner or later I was bound to fall in, and go floundering along, unable to get out again!

And the same thing applies to all gymnastic work. I have experimented with a dozen different systems of exercises, and with all kinds of water treatments; I have used dumb-bells and Indian clubs and Swedish gymnastics, MacFadden's exercises in bed, and the Yogi breathing exercises, and more kinds of queer things than I can remember now; but for me there is only one solution of the problem, which is to have an antagonist. It may be a deer I am trying to shoot, or some trout I am trying to lure out of their holes; it may be some boys I am trying to beat at football or hockey, or it may be the game I know best and find most convenient, which is tennis. If it is tennis, then it has to be someone who can make me work as hard as I know how; for if it is someone I can beat easily, why, before I have been playing ten minutes, I am busily working out the next chapter of a book, or answering letters I have just got in the mail.

Recently I came upon a book, "The Psychology of Relaxation," by Dr. Patrick, in which the theory of this is set forth. Civilized man is working his higher brain centers more than his body can stand; his brain is running away with him, absorbing a constantly increasing share of his energies. True relaxation is only possible where the higher brain centers are lulled, and the back lobes of the brain brought into activity. One of the means of doing this is alcohol, and that is why through the ages all races of men have craved to get drunk. There is a method which is harmless, and does not break down the system, and that is play. When we become really interested in play, we are as children, or as primitive man; we do all the things that our race used to do many ages ago; we hunt and fight, we pit our wits against the wits of our enemies, and struggle with desperation to get the better of them. If our play is physical play, if we are absorbed in a game or bodily contest, then we are exerting and developing all those portions of us which civilization tends to atrophy and deaden.

There are people who will dispute with you about Socialism, and ask, how we are going to provide incentives if we do away with wage slavery. When you tell them that activity is natural to human beings, and that if there were no work, men and women would have to make some, they shake their heads mournfully and tell you about the problem of "human nature." But consider games and sports: men do not have to work their bodies, yet they go out and deliberately hunt for trouble! They invent themselves subtle and complicated games, and are not content until they find people who can beat them at it, or at any rate can make them work to the limit of their strength, until they are in a dripping perspiration and thoroughly exhausted! I may be too optimistic about "human nature," but I believe that this is the attitude every normal human being takes toward the powers, both mental and physical, which he possesses; he wants to use them, and for all they are worth. If you don't believe it, just take any group of youngsters, give them a baseball and bat, turn them loose in a vacant lot, and watch them "choose up sides" and fall to work, screaming and shouting in wild excitement! There are some races of the earth which do not yet know baseball, but the Filipinos and the Japanese have learned it, and even the war-worn "Poilus" and the supercilious "Tommies" condescended to experiment with it. And if you think it is only physical competition that young human animals enjoy, try them at putting on a play, or printing a magazine, or conducting a debate, or building a house—anything whatever that involves healthy competition, and is related to the big things of life, but without being for the profit of some exploiter! Get clear the plain and simple distinction between work and play: play is what you want to do, while work is what the profit system makes you do!

CHAPTER XXV

THE FASTING CURE

(Deals with nature's own remedy for disease, and how to make use of it.)

We have next to consider the various human ailments, what causes them, and how they can be remedied. As it happens, I know of a cure that comes pretty near being that impossible thing, a "cure-all." At any rate, it is so far ahead of all other cures, that a discussion of it will cover three-fourths of the subject.

When I was a boy living in New York, there was a man by the name of Dr. Tanner, who took a forty-day fast. He was on public exhibition at the time, and was supposed to be watched day and night; the newspapers gave a great deal of attention to the story, and crowds used to come to gaze at him. I remember very well the conversations I heard about the matter. People were quite sure that it couldn't be true. The man must be getting something to eat on the sly; he must have some nourishment in the water he drank; no human being could fast more than five or six days without starving to death.

In the year 1910 I published in the United States and England a magazine article telling how on several occasions I had fasted ten or twelve days, and what I had accomplished by it. I found that I had the same difficulty to confront as old Dr. Tanner; I received scores of letters from people who called me a "faker," and I read scores of newspaper editorials to the same effect. The New York Times published a dispatch about three young ladies on Long Island who were trying a three-day fast, and the Times commented editorially to the effect that these young ladies were "the victims of a shallow and unscrupulous sensationalist."

The notion that human beings can perish for lack of food in a few days is deeply rooted in people's minds. Recently a group of eleven Irishmen in jail set to work to starve themselves to death, as a protest against British rule in their country. Day after day the newspapers reported the news from Cork prison, and at about the twentieth day they began to state that the prisoners were dying, that the priest had been sent for, that their relatives were gathered on the prison steps. Day after day such reports continued, through the thirties, and the forties, and the fifties, and the sixties, and the seventies. One man died on the eighty-eighth day, and MacSwiney died on the seventy-fourth. The other nine gave up after ninety-four days and were all restored to health. I watched carefully the newspaper and magazine comment on this incident, yet I did not see a single remark on the medical aspects of it; I could not discover that scientific men had learned anything whatever about the ability of the body to go without food for long periods.

Get this clear at the outset: Nobody ever "starved to death" in less than two months, and it is possible for a fat person to go without food for as long as three or four months. People who "starve to death" in shorter times do not die of starvation, but of fright. The first time I fasted happened to be at the time of the Messina earthquake. I was walking about, perfectly serene and happy, having been without food for three days, and I read in my newspaper how the rescue ships had reached Messina, and found the population ravenous, in the agonies of starvation, some of the people having been without food for seventy-two hours! (It sounds so much worse, you see, when you state it in hours.)

The second point to get clear is that the fast is a physiological process; that is to say, it is something which nature understands and carries through in her own serene and efficient way. When you take a fast, you are not carrying out a freak notion of your own, or of mine; you are discovering a lost instinct. Every cat and dog knows enough not to take food when it is ill; it is only in hospitals conducted by modern medical science that the custom prevails of serving elaborate "trays" to invalids. I remember a story about a man who made himself a reputation and a fortune by curing the pet dogs of the rich. These beautiful little creatures, which sleep between silken covers, and have several servants to wait upon them, and are fed from gold and silver dishes upon rich and elaborately cooked foods, fall victim to as many diseases as their mistresses, and they would be brought to this specialist, who conducted his dog hospital in an old brickyard. In each one of the compartments of the brick kiln he would shut up a dog with a supply of fresh water, a crust of stale bread, a piece of bacon rind, and the sole of an old shoe; and after a few days he would go back and find that the dog had eaten the crust of bread, and then he would write to the owner that the dog was on the high road to recovery. He would go back a few days later and find that the dog had eaten the piece of bacon rind, and then he would write that the dog was very nearly cured. He would wait until the dog had eaten the piece of shoe leather, and then he would write that the dog was completely cured, and the owner might come and take it away.

Just what is the process of the fast cure? I do not pretend to know positively. I can only make guesses, and wait for science to investigate. I believe that the main source of the diseases of civilized man is improper nutrition, and the clogging of the system with food poisons in various stages. And when you fast you do two things: first, you stop entirely the fresh supply of those food poisons, and second, you allow the whole of the body's digestive and assimilative tract to rest—to go to sleep, as it were—so that all the body's energy may go to other organs. The body carries with it at all times a surplus store of nutriment, which can be taken up and used by the blood stream, apparently with much less trouble than is required to convert fresh food to the body's uses. In other words, the body can feed on its own tissues more easily than it can feed from the stomach. In the fast you may lose anywhere from half a pound to two pounds in weight per day, and this will be taken, first from your store of fat, and then from your muscular tissues. Every part of your muscular tissue will be taken, before anything is taken from your vital organs, your nerves or your blood-stream. So long as there is a particle of muscular material left, so long as you can make even the slightest movement of one finger, you are still fasting, and it is only when your muscular tissue is all gone that you begin at last to starve. So far as I know, the cases of MacSwiney and the other Irishman are the only cases on record where fasters have died of starvation.

What the body does during the fast is quite plain, and can be told by many symptoms. It begins a thorough house-cleaning, throwing out poisonous material by every channel. The perspiration and the breath become offensive, the tongue becomes heavily coated, so that you can scrape the material off with a knife. I have heard vegetarians explain this by saying that when the body is living off its own tissues, it is following a cannibal diet; but that is all nonsense, because you can live on meat exclusively, and quickly satisfy yourself that none of these symptoms occurs. It is evident that the body is taking advantage of the opportunity to get rid of waste products; and this will go on for ten days, for twenty days, in some cases for as long as forty or fifty days; and then suddenly occurs a strange thing: in spite of the "cannibal diet" the symptoms all come to a sudden end. The tongue clears, the breath becomes sweet, the appetite suddenly awakens.

During the period of a normal fast you lose all interest in food. You almost forget that there is such a thing as eating; you can look at food without any more desire for it than you have to swallow marbles and carpet tacks. But then suddenly appetite returns, as I have explained, and you find that you can think of nothing but food. This is what students of the subject describe as a "complete fast," and while I do not want to go to extremes and say that the "complete fast" will cure every case of every disease, I can certainly say this: in the letters which have come to me from people who tried the fast at my suggestion, there are cases of every kind of common disease. In my book, "The Fasting Cure," I give the results in cases reported to me after the publication of my first magazine article. I quote two paragraphs:

"The total number of fasts taken was 277, and the average number of days was six. There were 90 of five days or over, 51 of ten days or over, and six of 30 days or over. Out of the 119 person who wrote to me, 100 reported benefit, and 17 no benefit. Of these 17 about half give wrong breaking of the fast as the reason for the failure. In cases where the cure had not proved permanent, about half mentioned that the recurrence of the trouble was caused by wrong eating, and about half of the rest made this quite evident by what they said. Also it is to be noted that in the cases of the 17 who got no benefit, nearly all were fasts of only three or four days.

"Following is the complete list of diseases benefited—45 of the cases having been diagnosed by physicians: indigestion (usually associated with nervousness), 27; rheumatism, 5; colds, 8; tuberculosis, 4; constipation, 14; poor circulation, 3; headaches, 5; anaemia, 3; scrofula, 1; bronchial trouble, 5; syphilis, 1; liver trouble, 5; general debility, 5; chills and fever, 1; blood poisoning, 1; ulcerated leg, 1; neurasthenia, 6; locomotor ataxia, 1; sciatica, 1; asthma, 2; excess of uric acid, 1; epilepsy, 1; pleurisy, 1; impaction of bowels, 1; eczema, 2; catarrh, 6; appendicitis, 3; valvular disease of heart, 1; insomnia, 1; gas poisoning, 1; grippe, 1; cancer, 1."

There are many diseases with many causes, and some yield more quickly than others to the fast. In the first group I put the diseases of the digestive and alimentary tract. Stomach and bowel troubles, and the nervous disorders occasioned by these, stop almost immediately when you fast. Next come disorders of the blood-stream, which are generally a second stage of digestive troubles. Everything immediately due to impurities of the blood, pimples, boils, and ulcers, inflammation, badly healing wounds, etc., respond to a few days of fasting as to the magic touch of the old-time legends. When it comes to diseases caused by germ infections, you have a double aspect of the problem, and must have a double method of attack. I would not like to say that fasting could cure such a disease as sleeping sickness, to the germs of which our systems are not accustomed, and against which they may well be helpless. On the other hand, in the case of common infections, such as colds and sore throats, the fast is again the touch of magic. Having been plagued a great deal by these ailments in past times, I am accustomed to say that I would not trade my knowledge of fasting for everything else that I know about health.

The first thing you must do if you want to take a fast is to read the literature on the subject and make up your mind that the experiment will do you no injury. You should also try to get your relatives to make up their minds, because you are nervous when you are fasting, and cannot withstand the attacks of the people around you, who will go into a panic and throw you into a panic. As I said before, it is quite possible for people to die of panic, but I do not believe that anybody ever died of a fast. I have known of two or three cases of people dying while they were fasting, but I feel quite certain that the fast did not cause their death; they would have died anyhow. You must bear in mind that among the people who try the fast, a great many are in a desperate condition; some have been given up by the doctors, and if now and then one of these should die, we may surely say that they died in spite of the fast, and not because of it. There is no physician who can save every patient, and it would be absurd to expect this. I have read scores of letters from people who were at the point of death from such "fatal" diseases as Bright's disease, sclerosis of the liver, and fatty degeneration of the heart, and were literally snatched out of the jaws of death by beginning a fast. I would not like to guess just what percentage of dying people in our hospitals might be saved if the doctors would withdraw all food from them, but I await with interest the time when medical science will have the intelligence to try that simple experiment and report the results.

Just the other day in the Los Angeles county jail, a chiropractor went on hunger strike, as a protest against imprisonment, and he fasted 41 days. Then he broke his fast, the reason being given that his pulse was down to 54, and he was afraid of dying. I smiled to myself. The normal pulse is 70. I have taken my pulse many times at the end of a ten-day fast, and it has been as low as 32, and I am not dead yet, and if I wait to die from the symptoms of a fast, I expect to live a long time indeed!

The first time I fasted, I felt very weak, and lay around and hardly cared to lift my head; if I walked from my bed to the lawn, I was tired in the legs. But since then I have grown used to fasting. I have fasted for a week probably twenty or thirty times, and on such occasions I have gone about my business as if nothing were happening. Of course I would not try to play tennis, or to climb a mountain, but it is a fact that on the seventh day of a fast in New York, I climbed the five or six flights of stairs to the top of the Metropolitan Opera House, and felt no ill effects from doing this. I climbed slowly, and was careful not to tire myself. The simple rule is not to have anything that you must do on the fast, and then do what you feel like doing. Lie down and rest, and read a book, and take as much exercise as you find you enjoy. Keep your mind quiet and free from worries, and lock out of the house everybody who tells you that your heart is going to stop beating in the next few minutes, and that you must have an injection of strychnine to start it, and some beefsteak and fried onions to "restore your strength." Give yourself up to the care of your wise old mother nature, who will attend to your heart just as securely and serenely as she attended to it in the days before you were born.

By fasting I mean that you take no food whatever. I know some nature cure teachers who practice what they call a "fruit fast." All I know is that if I eat nothing but fruit, I soon have my stomach boiling with fermentation, and also I suffer with hunger; whereas, if I take a complete fast, I promptly forget all about food. You must drink all the water you can on the fast. This helps nature with her house-cleaning; it is well to drink a glass of water every half hour at least. Do not try to go without water, and then write me that the fasting cure is a failure. Also please do not write and ask me if it will be fasting if you take just a little crackers and milk, or some soup, or something else that you think doesn't count!

I recommend a dose of laxative to clean out the system at the beginning of a fast, because the bowels are apt to become sluggish at once, and the quicker you get the system cleansed, the better. It does no good to take laxatives if you are going to pile in more food, but if you are going to fast, that is a different matter. You should take a full warm enema every day during the fast, so long as it brings any results. There are some people whose bowels are so frightfully clogged that I have known the enema to bring results even in the second and third weeks. On the other hand, if there is no solid matter to be removed, a small enema every day will suffice. Take a warm bath every day; and needless to say, you should get all the fresh air you can, and should sleep as much as you can. You may have difficulty in sleeping, because the fast is apt to make you nervous and wakeful. I have known people who could not fast because they could not sleep, and I have taught them a little trick, to put a hot water bottle at the feet, and another on the abdomen, to draw the blood away from the head. So they would quickly fall asleep, and they got great benefit from their fasts.

You should supply yourself with good music if you can, and with plenty of good reading matter. You will be amazed to find how active your mind becomes; perhaps you had never known before what a mind you had. Your blood has always been so clogged with food poisons that you didn't know you could think. My three act play, "The Nature Woman," was conceived and written in two days and a half on a fast; but I do not recommend this kind of thing—on the contrary, I strongly urge against it, because if you work your brain on a fast, you do not get the good from your fast, and do not recover so quickly. Put off all your problems until you have got your health back, and seek only to divert your mind while fasting.

CHAPTER XXVI

BREAKING THE FAST

(Discusses various methods of building up the body after a fast, especially the milk diet.)

There remains the question of how to break the fast, and this is the most important part of the problem. You may undo all the good of your fast by breaking it wrong, and you are a thousand times as apt to kill yourself then, as while you are fasting. When your hunger comes back, it comes back with a rush, and some people have not the will power to control it.

I do not advocate a complete fast in any case except of serious chronic disease, and then only under the advice of someone with experience; but I advocate a short fast of a week or ten days for almost every common ailment, and I know that such a fast will help, even where it may not completely cure. You may go on fasting so long as you are quiet and happy; but when you find you are becoming too weak for comfort, or for the peace of mind of your family physician and your friends, you may break your fast, and show them that it is possible to restore your strength and body weight, and then they won't bother so much when you try it again! Take nothing but liquid foods in the breaking of a fast; I recommend the juices of fruits and tomatoes, also meat broths. If you have fasted a week or two, take a quarter of a glass; if you have fasted a month, take a tablespoonful, and wait and see what the results are. Remember that your whole alimentary tract is out of action, and give it a chance to start up slowly. Take small quantities of liquid food every two hours for the first day. Then you can begin taking larger quantities, and on the next day you can try some milk, or a soft poached egg, or the pulp of cooked apples or prunes. Do not take any solid food until you are quite sure you can digest it, and then take only a very little. Do not take any starchy food until the third day.

I have known people to break these rules. I knew a man who broke his fast on hamburg steak, and had to be helped out with a stomach pump. Once I broke a week's fast with a plate of rich soup, because I was at a friend's house and there was nothing else, and I yielded to the claims of hospitality, and made myself ill and had to fast for several days longer.

The easiest way to break a fast is upon a milk diet. I have seen hundreds of people take this diet, and very few who did not get benefit. The first time I fasted, which was twelve days, I lost 17 pounds, and I took the milk diet for 24 days thereafter, and gained 32 pounds. I took it at MacFadden's Sanitarium, where I had every attention. Since then, I have many times tried to take a milk diet by myself, but have never been able to get it to agree with me. I do not know how to explain this fact; I state it, to show how hard it is to lay down general rules. On the milk diet you take into your system two or three times as much food as you can assimilate, and this is a violation of all my diet rules; but it appears that the bacteria which thrive in milk produce lactic acid, which is not harmful to the system, and if you do not take other foods you may safely keep the system flooded with milk.

After a fast you should begin with small quantities of milk, and by the third day you may be taking a full glass of warm milk every half hour or every twenty minutes, until you have taken seven or eight quarts per day. It is better to take it warm, but sometimes people take it just as well without warming. Dr. Porter, who has a book on the milk diet, insists upon complete rest, and makes his patients stay in bed. MacFadden, on the other hand, recommends gymnastics in the morning before the milk, and during the afternoon he recommends a rest from the milk for a couple of hours, followed by abdominal exercises to keep the bowels open. This is very important during a fast, because you are taking great quantities of material into your system and it must not be permitted to clog. Therefore take an enema daily, if necessary to a free movement. Also take a warm bath daily. Take the juice of oranges and lemons if you crave them.

Upon one thing everyone who has had experience with the milk diet agrees, and that is the necessity of absolute mental rest. If you become excited, or nervous, or angry on a milk diet, you may turn all the contents of your stomach into hard curds, and may put yourself into convulsions. The wonderful thing about the milk diet is the state of physical and mental bliss it makes possible. It is the ideal way of breaking a fast, because it leaves you no chance to get hungry; you have all the food you want, and your system is bathed in happiness, a sense of peace and well-being which is truly marvelous and not to be described. You gain anywhere from half a pound to two pounds a day, and you feel that you have never before in your life known what perfect health could be. The fast sets you a new standard, you discover how nature meant you to enjoy life, and never again are you content with that kind of half existence with which you managed to worry along before you discovered this remedy.

But let me hasten to add that I do not recommend the fast as a regular habit of life. The fast is an emergency measure, to enable the body to cleanse itself and to cure disease. When you have got your body clean and free from disease, it is your business to keep it that way, and you should apply your reason to the problem of how to live so that you will not have to fast. If you find that you continue to have ailments, then you must be eating wrongly, or overworking, or committing some other offense against nature; either that, or else you must have some organic trouble—a bone in your spine out of place, as the osteopaths tell you, or your eyes out of focus, or your appendix twisted and infected. I do not claim that the fasting cure will supplant the surgeons and the oculists and the dentists. It will not mend your bones if you break them, and it will not repair your teeth that are already decayed; but it will help to keep your teeth from decaying in the future, and it will help you to prepare for a surgical operation, and to recover from it more quickly. I had to undergo an operation for rupture a couple of years ago, and I fasted for two days before the operation, and for three days after it, and I had no particle of nausea from the ether, and was able to tend to my mail the day after the operation.

There is one disease for which I hesitate to recommend the fast, and that is tuberculosis, because I have been told of cases in which the patient lost weight and did not recover it. However, in my tabulation of 277 cases, you will note four cases of tuberculosis, and in my book is given a letter from a patient who claimed great benefit. If I had the misfortune to contract tuberculosis, I would take a three or four day fast, followed by a milk diet for a long period. The milk diet is pleasant to take, and it cannot possibly do any harm. If it did not effect a cure, I would try the Salisbury treatment— that is, lean meat ground up and medium cooked, and nothing else, except an abundance of hot water between meals. Prof. Irving Fisher wrote me that there is urgent need of experiment to determine proper diet in tuberculosis; and until these experiments have been made, we can only grope. I am quite sure that the "stuffing system," ordinarily used by doctors, is a tragic mistake.

In the case of any other disease whatever, even though I might take medical or surgical treatment, I would supplement this by a fast, because there is no kind of treatment which does not succeed better with the blood in good condition. In the case of emergencies, accidents, wounds, etc., I would rest assured that recovery would be more prompt if I were fasting. When David Graham Phillips was shot, I wrote a letter to the New York Call, saying that his doctors had killed him, because they had fed him while he was lying in a critical condition in the hospital. To take nutriment into the body under such circumstances is the greatest of blunders.

The fast will help children, just as it helps adults, only they do not need to fast so long. It will help the aged and make them feel young. (You need not be afraid to fast, no matter how old you are.) It is, of course, an immediate cure for fatness, and strange as it may seem, it is also a cure for unnatural thinness. People with ravenous appetites are just as apt to be thin as to be fat, because it is not what you eat that builds up your body, but only what you assimilate, and if you eat too much, you can make it impossible to assimilate anything properly. If you take a fast and break it carefully, your body will come to its normal weight, and all your functions to their normal activity.

A physician wrote me, taking me to task for listing among the cures reported in my tabulation a case of locomotor ataxia. This disease, he explained, is caused because a portion of a nerve has been entirely destroyed, and it is a disease that is absolutely and positively and forever incurable. I answered that I knew this to be the teaching of present day medical science, but I invited him to consider for a moment what happens in nature. When a crab loses a claw, we do not take it as a matter of course that the crab must go about with one claw for the balance of its life; nature will make that crab another claw. Man has lost the power of replacing a lost leg, but he stills retains the power of replacing tissue which has been cut away by a surgeon's knife, and medical science takes this as a matter of course. How shall anybody say that nature has forever lost the power of rebuilding a bit of nervous tissue? How shall anyone say that if the blood-stream is cleansed of poisons, and the energy of the whole body restored, one of the results may not be the repairing of a broken nerve connection? I invite my readers who have ailments, and especially I invite all medical men among my readers, to make a fair test of the fasting cure. The results will surprise them, and they will quickly be forced to revise their methods of treating illness.

XXVII

DISEASES AND CURES

(Discusses some of the commoner human ailments, and what is known about their cause and cure.)

I begin with the commonest of all troubles, known as a "cold." This name implies that the cause of the trouble lies in exposure or chill. All the grandmothers of the world are agreed about this. They have a phrase—or at least they had it when I was a boy: "You will catch your death." Every time I went out in the rain, every time I played with wet feet, or sat in a draft, or got under a cold shower, I would hear the formula, "You will catch your death."

And, on the other hand, there are the "health cranks," who declare vehemently that the name "cold" is a misnomer and a trap for people's thoughts. Cold has nothing to do with it, they say, and point to arctic explorers who frequently get frozen to death, but do not "catch cold" until they get back into the warm rooms of civilization. As for drafts, the "health cranks" aver that a draft is merely "fresh air moving"; which is supposed to settle the matter. However, when you come to think about it, you realize that a cyclone is likewise merely "fresh air moving," so you have not decided the question by a phrase.

While I was writing these chapters on health I contracted a severe cold—which was a joke on me. The history of this cold is as clear in my mind as anything human can be, and it will serve for an illustration, showing how much truth the grandmothers have on their side, and how much the "health cranks" have.

To begin with, I had been overworking. All sorts of appeals come to me; hundreds of people write me letters, and I cannot bear to leave them unanswered. I accepted calls to speak, and invitations where I had to eat a lot of stuff of which my reason disapproves; so one morning I woke up with a slight sore throat. I fasted all day, and by evening felt all right. But there came another call, and I consented to take a long automobile ride on a cold and rainy night, and when I got back home, after five or six hours, I was thoroughly chilled, and my "cold" came on during the night.

This explanation will, I imagine, be satisfactory to all the grandmothers of the world. All the dear, good grandmothers know that an automobile ride on a cold, rainy night is enough to give any man "his death." But listen, grandmothers! I have lain out watching for deer all night in the late fall, with only a thin blanket to cover me, and gotten up so stiff with cold that I could hardly move; yet I did not "catch cold." When I was a youth, I have ridden a bicycle twenty miles to the beach in April, with snow on the ground, and plunged into the surf and swam, and then ridden home again. I have bathed in the sea when I had to run a quarter of a mile in a bathing suit along a frost-covered pier, and with an icy wind blowing through my bones; yet I never took cold from that, and never got anything but a feeling of exhilaration. So it must be that there is some reason why exposure causes colds at one time and not at another.

The explanation takes you over to the "health cranks." They understand that your blood-stream must be clogged, your bodily tone reduced by bad air and lack of exercise, and more especially by over-eating, or by an improperly balanced diet. But then most of them go to extremes, and insist that the automobile ride and the chilled condition of my body had nothing to do with my cold. But I know otherwise—I have watched the thing happen so often. In times when I was run down, the slightest exposure would cause me a cold, literally in a few minutes. I have got myself a sore throat going out to the wood-pile on a winter day with nothing on my head. I have got a cold by sitting still with wet feet, or by sitting in a draft on a warm summer day, when I had been perspiring a little. How to explain this I am not sure, but my guess is that you drive the blood away from the surface of the body at a time when it is weakened and exposed to infection, and you drive away the army of the white corpuscles, and give the battlefield of your body to the germs.

I know there are nature curists who argue that germs have nothing to do with disease; but they have never been able to convince me—germs are too real, and too many, and too easy to watch. If you leave a piece of meat exposed to the air in warm temperature, the germs in the air will settle upon it and begin to feed upon it and to multiply; the meat, being dead, is powerless to protect itself. But your nose and throat are also meat, and just as good food for the germs. The only difference is that this meat is alive, there is a living blood-stream circulating through it, and several score billions of the body's own kind of germs, the blood corpuscles. If these blood corpuscles are sound and properly nourished, and are brought to the place of infection, they are able to destroy all the common germs; so it is that you do not have diseases, but instead have health. But your health always implies a struggle of your organism against other organisms, and it is the business of your reason to watch your body and give all the help you can in protecting it. Coughs and colds, sore throats and headaches, are the first warnings that your defenses are being weakened. As a rule these ailments are not serious in themselves, but they are signs of a wrong condition, and if you neglect this condition, pretty soon you will find that you have to deal with something deadly.

My cure for a cold is to take an enema and a laxative, eat nothing for twenty-four hours, and drink plenty of water. If you have a severe cold or sore throat, you will be wise to lie in bed for a day or two, by an open window. You may also use sprays and gargles if you wish, but you will find them of little use, because the germs are deep in your mucous membranes, and cannot all be reached from the outside. In the old sad days of my ignorance I would get a cold, and go to the doctor, and have my throat and nose pumped full of black and green and yellow and purple liquids, which did me absolutely no good whatever; the cold would stay on for two or three weeks, sometimes for eight or ten weeks, and I would be miserable, utterly desperate. I was dying by inches, and not one of the doctors could tell me why.

The next most common ailment is a headache, and this means poisons in your blood-stream. It may be from improper diet, from alcohol, or drugs, or bad air, or nervous excitement. If it is none of these things, then you should begin to look for some organic difficulty, eye-strain, for example, or perhaps defects in the spine. The osteopaths and the chiropractors specialize on the spine, and have made important discoveries. Their doctrine is, in brief, that the nervous force which directs the blood-stream is carried to the organs of the body by nerves which leave the spinal cord through openings between the vertebrae. If any of these openings are pinched, you have a diminished nerve supply, which means ill-health in that part of the body to which the nerve leads. That such trouble can be corrected by straightening the bones of the spine, seems perfectly reasonable; but like most people with a new idea, the discoverers proceed to carry it to absurd extremes. I have before me an official chiropractic pamphlet which states that vertebral displacement is "the physical and perpetuating cause of ninety-five per cent of all cases of disease; the remaining five per cent being due to subluxations of other skeletal segments." Naturally people who believe this will devote nearly all their study to the bones and the nervous system. But surely, there are other parts of your body which are necessary besides bones and nerves! And what if some of these parts happen to be malformed or defective? What if your eyes do not focus properly, and you are continually wearing out the optic nerve, thus giving yourself headaches and neurasthenia? What if you have an appendix that has been twisted and malformed from birth, and is a center of infection so long as it remains in the body?

Several years ago I had an experience with the appendix, from which I learned something about one of the commonest of human ailments, constipation, or sluggishness of the bowels. This is a cause of innumerable chronic ailments grouped under the head of auto-intoxication, or the poisoning of the body by the absorption into the system of the products of fermentation and decay in the bowels. The bowels should move freely two or three times every day, and the movements should be soft. I suffered from constipation for some twenty years, and tried, I think, every remedy known both to science and to crankdom. In the beginning the doctors gave me drugs which by irritating the intestinal walls cause them to pour out quantities of water, and hurry the irritating substances down the intestinal tract. That is all right for an emergency; if you have swallowed a poison, or food which is spoiled, or if you have overeaten and are ill, get your system cleaned out by any and every device. But if you habitually swallow mild poisons, which is what all laxatives are, you weaken the intestinal tract, and you have to take more and more of these poisons, and you get less results. We may set down as positive the statement that drugs are not a remedy for constipation.

Next comes diet. Eat the rough and bulky foods, say the nature curists, and stimulate the intestinal walls to activity. I tried that. I listened to the extreme enthusiasts, and boiled whole wheat and ate it, and consumed quantities of bran biscuit, and of a Japanese seaweed which Dr. Kellogg prepares, and of petroleum oil, and even the skins of oranges, which are most uncomfortable eating, I assure you. I would eat things like this until I got myself a case of diarrhea—and so was cured of constipation for a time!

Strange as it may seem to you, there are even people who tell you to eat sand. I listened to them, and ate many quarts.

Then there is exercise. MacFadden taught me a whole series of exercises for developing the muscles of the abdominal walls and the back, which are greatly neglected by civilized man. The fundamental cause of constipation is a sluggish life, and to exercise our bodies is a duty; but to me it was always an agony of boredom to lie on a bed and wiggle my abdomen for a quarter of an hour. The same thing applies to hot water treatments, which are effective, but a nuisance and a waste of time. I never could keep them up except when I was in trouble.

Three or four years ago I began to notice a continual irritating pain in my right side, which I quickly realized must lie in the appendix. I tried massage, and hot and cold water treatments, and my favorite remedy, a week's fast. The pain disappeared, but it returned, so finally I decided, to the dismay of my physical culture friends, to have the appendix out. For years I had been reading the statements of nature curists, that the appendix is an important and vital part of the body, which pours an oil or something into the intestinal tract, and so helps to prevent constipation. Well, evidently my appendix wasn't doing its job, so I took it to a good surgeon. What I found was that it had been twisted and malformed from birth, so that it was a center of continuous infection. From the time I had that operation, I have never had to think about the subject of constipation. This experience suggests to me how easy it is for people to make statements about health which have no relationship to facts.

I do not recommend promiscuous surgery, and I perfectly well realize that if human beings would take proper care of their health, the great proportion of surgical operations would be unnecessary. I realize, also, that surgeons get paid by the job, and therefore have a money interest in operating, and it is perfectly futile to expect that none of them will ever be influenced by the profit motive. Nevertheless, it is true that sometimes surgical operations are necessary, and that by standing a little temporary inconvenience you can save yourself a life-time of discomfort.

Take, for example, rupture. The human body has here a natural weakness, from which there results a dangerous and uncomfortable affliction. Hundreds of thousands of men are going around all their lives wearing elaborate and expensive trusses which are almost, if not entirely useless, and trying advertised "cures" which are entirely fakes. An operation takes an hour or two, and two or three weeks in bed, and when our government drafted its young men into the army and found that fourteen in every thousand of them had rupture, it shipped them into the hospitals wholesale and sewed them up. It happens that rupture affords one case where scar tissue is stronger than natural tissue, and there were practically no returns from the great number of army cases.

Likewise you find extreme statements repeated concerning the evils of vaccination; but if you will read Parkman's "History of the Jesuits in North America," you will see the horrible conditions under which the Indians lived in the United States—noble savages, you understand, entirely uncontaminated by civilized white men, and whole populations regularly wiped out every few years by epidemics of smallpox. That these epidemics ceased was due to the discovery that by infecting the body with a mild form of the disease, it could be made to develop substances which render it immune to the deadly form. Here in California we have a law which makes vaccination for school children optional, and so we may some day have another epidemic to test the theories of the anti-vaccinationists.

I know, of course, the dreadful stories of people who have been given syphilis and other diseases by impure vaccines. I don't know whether such stories are true; but I do know that people who live in houses are sometimes killed by earthquakes and by lightning, yet we do not cease to live in houses because of this chance. It seems to me that the remedy for such vaccination evils is not to abolish vaccination, but to take more care in the manufacture of our vaccines.

This danger is removed by using vaccines which are sterile, and are made especially for each person. Germs are taken from the sick person, and injected into an animal. The body of the animal develops with great rapidity the "anti-bodies" necessary to resistance to the germs; and as these "anti-bodies" are chemical products, not affected by heat, we can take a serum from the animal, sterilize it, and then inject it into the system of the patient, thus increasing resistance to the disease. I admit that the best way to increase such resistance is to take care of your health; but sometimes we confront an emergency, and must use emergency remedies. We have serums that really cure diphtheria and meningitis, and one that will prevent lock-jaw; anyone who has ever seen with his own eyes how the deadly membranes of diphtheria melt away as a result of an injection, will be less dogmatic about the efforts of science to combat disease.

Of course it is much pleasanter if you can destroy the source of the disease, and keep it from getting into the human body. Every few years the southern part of our country used to be devastated by yellow fever epidemics. Every kind of weird and fantastic remedy was tried; people would go around with sponges full of vinegar hung under their noses; they would burn the clothing and bedding of those who died of the disease; they would wear gloves when they went shopping, so as not to touch the money with their hands. But at last medical experimenters traced the disease to a certain kind of mosquito, and now, if we drain the swamps and screen our houses and stay in doors after sundown, we do not get yellow fever, nor malaria either. In the same way, if we keep our bodies clean with soap and hot water, we do not get bitten by lice, and so do not die of typhus. If we take pains with our drains and water supply, so that human excrement does not get into it, and if we destroy the filth-carrying housefly, we do not have epidemics of typhoid.

But under conditions of battle it is not possible for men to take these precautions, and so when they go into the army they get a dose of typhoid serum. And this illustrates the difference between a true or hygienic remedy for disease, and a temporary or emergency remedy. If you say that you want to abolish war, and with it the need for typhoid vaccination, I cheerfully agree with you in this. All that I am trying to do is to point out the folly of flying to extremes, and rejecting any remedy which may help. What is the use of making the flat statement that vaccinations and serums never aid in the cure of disease, when any man can see with his own eyes the proof that they do? In the Spanish war, before typhoid vaccination, many times more soldiers died of this disease than died of bullets; but in the late war there was practically no typhoid at all in the army camps. On the other hand, it was noticed that the men who had just come in, and who therefore had just been vaccinated, were considerably more susceptible to influenza; which shows that vaccination does reduce the body condition for a time. The reader may say that in this case I am trying to sit on both sides of the fence; but the truth is that I am trying to keep an open mind, and to consider all the facts, and to avoid making rash statements.

One of the statements you hear most frequently is that drugs can never remedy disease, or help in remedying it. Now, I abhor the drugging system of the orthodox medical men; I have talked with them, and heard them talk with one another, and I know that they will mix up half a dozen different substances, in the vague hope that some one of them will have some effect. Even when they know definitely the effects they are producing, they are in many cases merely suppressing symptoms. On the other hand, however, it is a fact that medical science has had for a generation or two a specific which destroys the germs of one disease in the blood, without at the same time injuring the blood itself. That disease is malaria, and the drug is quinine. Of course, the way to avoid malaria is to drain the swamps; but you cannot do that all at once, nor can you always screen your house and stay in at sundown. When you first go into a country, you have no house to screen, and some emergency will certainly arise that exposes you to mosquito bites. So you will need quinine, and will be foolish not to use it, and know how to use it.

Recently medical chemists discovered another remedy, this time for syphilis. It is called salvarsan, and while it does not always cure, it frequently does. In laboratories today men are working over the problem of constructing a combination of molecules which will destroy the germ of sleeping sickness, without at the same time injuring the blood. If they find it, they will save hundreds of millions of lives. I do not see why we cannot recognize such a possibility, while at the same time making use of physical culture, of diet and fasting.

When the manuscript of this book was sent to the printer, there appeared in this place a paragraph telling of the work of Dr. Albert Abrams of San Francisco, in the diagnosis and cure of disease by means of radio-active vibrations. As the book is going to press, the writer finds himself in San Francisco, attending Dr. Abrams' clinics; and so he finds it possible to give a more extended account of some fascinating discoveries, which seem destined to revolutionize medical science. If I were to tell all that I have seen with my own eyes in the last twelve days, I fear the reader would find his powers of credulity overstretched, so I shall content myself with trying to tell, in very sober and cautious language, the theory upon which Abrams is working, and the technic which he has evolved.

Modern science has demonstrated that all matter is simply the activity of electrons, minute particles of electric force. This is a statement which no present-day physicist would dispute. The best evidence appears to indicate that a molecule of matter is a minute reproduction of the universe, a system of electrons whirling about a central nucleus. No eye has ever beheld an electron, for it is billions of times smaller than anything the microscope makes visible; but we can see the effects of electronic activity, and all modern books of physics give photographs of such. It is possible to determine the vibration rates of electrons, and to Dr. Abrams occurred the idea of determining the vibration rates of diseased tissue and disease germs. He discovered that it was invariably the same; not merely does all cancerous material, for example, yield the same rate, but the blood of a person suffering from cancer yields that rate, at all times and under all circumstances. The vibration of cancer, of tuberculosis, of syphilis—each is different, uniform and invariable. Likewise in the blood are other vibrations, uniform and dependable, which reveal the sex and age of the patient, the virulence of the disease and the period of its duration—yes, and even the location in the body, if there be some definite infected area. So here is a modern miracle, an infallible device for the diagnosis of disease. Dr. Abrams does not have to see the patient; all he has to have is a drop of blood on a piece of white blotting paper, and he sits in his laboratory and tells all about it, and somewhere several thousand miles away—in Toronto or Boston or New Orleans—a surgeon operates and finds what he has been told is there!

And that is only the beginning of the wonder; because, says Abrams, if you know the vibration rate of the electrons of germs, you can destroy those germs. It used to be a favorite trick of Caruso to tap a glass and determine its musical note, and then sing that note at the glass and shatter it to bits. It is well known that horses, trotting swiftly on a bridge, have sometimes coincided in their step with the vibration of the bridge and thus have broken it down. On that same principle this wizard of the electron introduces into your body radio-activity of a certain rate—and shall I say that he cures cancer and syphilis and tuberculosis of many years standing in a few treatments? I will not say that, because you would not and could not believe me. I will content myself with telling what my wife and I have been watching, twice a day for the past twelve days.

The scene is a laboratory, with rows of raised seats at one side for the physicians who attend the clinic. There is a table, with the instruments of measurement, and Dr. Abrams sits beside it, and before him stands a young man stripped to the waist. The doctor is tapping upon the abdomen of this man, and listening to the sounds. You will find this the weirdest part of the whole procedure, for you will naturally assume that this young man is being examined, and will be dazed when some one explains that the patient is in Toronto or Boston or New Orleans, and that this young man's body is the instrument which the doctor uses in the determining of the vibration rates of the patient's blood. Dr. Abrams tried numerous instruments, but has been able to find nothing so sensitive to electronic activity as a human body. He explains to his classes that the spinal cord is composed of millions of nerve fibres of different vibration rates; hence a certain rate communicated to the body, is automatically sorted out, and appears on a certain precise spot of the body in the form of increased activity, increased blood pressure in the cells, and hence what all physicians know as a "dull area," which can be discovered by what is known as "percussion," a tapping with a finger. To map out these areas is merely a matter of long and patient experiment; and Abrams has been studying this subject for some twenty years—he is author of a text-book on what is known as the "reactions of Abrams." So now he provides the world with a series of maps of the human body; and he sits in front of his "subject," and his assistant places a specimen of blood in a little electrically connected box, and sets the rheostat at some vibration number —say fifty—and Dr. Abrams taps on a certain square inch of the abdomen of his "subject," and announces the dread word "cancer." Then he places the electrode on another part of the "subject's" body, and taps some more, and announces that it is cancer of the small intestine, left side; some more tapping, and he announces that its intensity is twelve ohms, which is severe; and pretty soon there is speeding a telegram to the physician who has sent this blood specimen, telling him these facts, and prescribing a certain vibration rate upon the "oscilloclast," the instrument of radio-activity which Dr. Abrams has devised.

Now, you watch this thing for an hour or two, and you say to yourself: "Here is either the greatest magician in the history of mankind, or else the greatest maniac." You may have come prepared for some kind of fraud, but you soon dismiss that, for you realize that this man is desperately in earnest about what he is doing, and so are all the physicians who watch him. So you seek refuge in the thought that he must be deluding himself and them, perhaps unconsciously. But you talk with these men, and discover that they have come from all over the country, and always for one reason—they had sent blood specimens to Abrams, and had found that he never made a mistake; he told them more from a few drops of the patient's blood than they themselves had been able to find out from the whole patient. And then into the clinic come the doctor's own patients—I must have heard sixty or eighty of them tell their story and many of them have been lifted from the grave. People ten years blind from syphilis who can see; people operated on several times for cancer and given up for dying; people with tumors on the brain, or with one lung gone from tuberculosis. It is literally a fact that when you have sat in Abrams' clinic for a week, all disease loses its terrors.

This, you see, is really the mastery of life. If we can measure and control the minute universe of the electron and the atom, we have touched the ultimate source of our bodily life. I might take chapters of this book to tell you of the strange experiments I have seen in this clinic—showing you, for instance, how these vibrations respond to thought, how by denying to himself the disease the patient can for a few moments cancel in his body the activity of the harmful germs; showing how the reactions differ in the different sexes and at different ages, and how they respond to different colors and different drugs. Abrams' method has revealed the secret of such efficacy as drugs possess—their work is done by their radio-activity, and not by their chemical properties. Also the problem of vaccination has been solved—for Abrams has discovered a dread new disease, which is bovine syphilis, originally caused in cattle by human inoculation, and now reintroduced in the human being by vaccination, and becoming the agent which prepares the soil of the body for such disorders as tuberculosis and cancer. And it appears that we can all be rendered immune to these diseases, by a few electronic vibrations, introduced into our bodies in childhood; so is opened up to our eyes a wonderful vision of a new race, purified and made fit for life. So here at last is science justified of her optimism, and our faith in human destiny forever vindicated. Take my advice, whoever you may be that are suffering, and find out about this new work and help to make it known to the world.

There are many romances of medical science, some of them fascinating as murder mysteries and big game hunting. Turn to McMasters' "History of the People of the United States" and read his account of the terrible epidemic of yellow fever in Philadelphia a hundred years ago; I have already referred to the weird and incredible things the people did in their effort to ward off this plague—sponges of vinegar under their noses and "fever fires" burning in the streets; and then a mosquito would fly up and bite them, and in a few hours they would be dead! Or what could be stranger than the tracing of the bubonic plague, which has cost literally billions of human lives, to a parasite in the blood of fleas which live on the bodies of rats! Or what could be more unexpected than the tracing of our rheumatic aches and twinges to the root canals of the teeth!

One of the common ailments which afflict poor humanity is rheumatism, a cause of endless suffering. It was supposed to be due to damp climate and exposure, and this is true to a certain extent, in the same way that colds are due to exposure. But the investigators realized that there must be some bodily condition rendering one susceptible, and they set to work to trace this condition down. The pains of rheumatism are caused by uric acid settling in the joints of the body. What causes the uric acid? Well, there is uric acid in red meat, so let us forbid rheumatic people to eat it! But this is overlooking the fact that the human body itself is a uric acid factory; and also the fact that uric acid taken into the stomach may not remain uric acid by the time it gets to the blood-stream. We know that you may eat a great deal of fruit acid without necessarily making acid blood. On the other hand, you can make acid blood by eating a lot of sugar! So you see it isn't as simple as it sounds.

Rheumatism has been traced to its lair, which is found to be the roots of the teeth. Here is a part of the body difficult to get at, and as a consequence of bad diet and unwholesome ways of living, infections will start there, and pus sacs be formed, and the poisons absorbed into the blood-stream and distributed through the body. The first thought is to draw the infected teeth; but that is a serious matter, because you need your teeth to chew your food. So the dentist has to go through a complicated process of opening up the tooth and cleaning out the root canals, and treating the infected spots at the roots. Then he has to fill the tooth all the way down to the roots, leaving no place for infection to gather. This, of course, takes time and costs money, and is one more illustration of the fact that there is one health law for the rich and another health law for the poor.

All the time that I write these chapters about health I feel guilty. I know that the wholesome food I recommend costs money, and I know that surgery and dentistry cost money—yes, even sunlight and fresh air and recreation; even a fast, because you have to rest while you take it, and you have to have a roof over your head, and warmth in winter time, and somebody to wait upon you when you are weak. I know that for a great many of the people who read what I write, all these things are impossible of attainment; I know that for the great majority of the common people the benefits of science do not exist. Science discovers how to prevent disease, but the discoveries are not applied, because the profit system controls the world, and the profit system wants the labor of the poor, regardless of what happens to their health. If the people fall ill, they are thrown upon the scrap heap, and the profit system finds others to take their place.

Take, for example, tuberculosis. Tuberculosis is a germ infection, but it practically never gets hold upon a human body except when the body is reduced by undernourishment and lack of fresh air. Tuberculosis, therefore, is a disease of slums and jails. It is definitely and indisputably a disease of poverty. It could be wiped off the face of the earth in a single generation; and the same is true of typhus and typhoid. There is another whole host of ailments which could be wiped out by measures of public hygiene, plus education. This includes all the infant diseases, and the deadly venereal diseases. But the profit system stands in the way; and so, in these closing paragraphs of this Book of the Body, I say that there is one disease which is the deadliest of all, and the source of all others, and that disease is poverty.

I know a certain physician to the rich, who is an honest and conscientious man. He said, "I loath my work. I am wasting my time. I am called in by these fat, over-fed rich people in their leisure class hotels, and what am I to say to them? Shall I say to them, 'You are living an abnormal life, and you can never be well until you cut out root and branch all your habits of self indulgence which are destroying you?' But no, I can't say that—not one time in a thousand. I am expected to be polite and serious, and to listen to them while they tell the long tiresome story of their symptoms, and I have to encourage them, and give them some temporary device that will remove some of the symptoms of their trouble."

And what should one say to this honest physician? Should one tell him to go and be a physician to the poor? Would he be any happier there? He could tell the poor the causes of their diseases, and they would listen patiently— they are trained to listen, and to accept what they are told. Here is a girl living in an inside bedroom in a tenement, and working ten or eleven hours a day in an unventilated factory, and she is ill with tuberculosis. The physician tells her that she needs plenty of fresh air and rest, and a lot of eggs and milk in her diet. He tells her that, and he knows that she has as much chance of carrying out his orders as of flying to the moon. Or maybe he comes upon a typhoid epidemic, and discovers, as happened to a friend of mine in Chicago, that there is defective plumbing in some houses owned by the political leader of the district. Or maybe it is a case of venereal disease, in a young man who was drafted into the army and turned loose amid the joys of Paris. Maybe it is just a commonplace, every-day story of a room full of school children, 22 per cent of them undernourished, as is the case in New York City, and the parents out of work a part of the time, and with no possibility in their lives of ever earning enough to feed the children properly. When you confront these universal facts of our present social order, you realize that the problem of disease is not merely a problem of the body, but is a problem of the mind as well; a problem of politics and religion and philosophy, of the whole way of thinking of the so-called civilized world. A book of health which did not point out these facts would be, not a book of health, but a book of sham.

But meantime, while we are trying to change the world's ideas, we have to live, and we can do our work better if we keep as well as possible. I have tried to point out the way; it is, as you can see, a matter in part of the body and in part of the mind. All the bodily régime here laid out has its basis in mental habits; all wise and wholesome ways of life can, at the age when our minds are plastic, be made into "second nature"—things which we do automatically, without effort or temptation to do otherwise. This is the real secret of true happiness in the conduct of our personal lives; to acquire self-control, to rule our desires and our passions, not harshly and spasmodically, but serenely, as one drives a car which he thoroughly understands. It is in vain that we preach freedom to men who have not this self-mastery; as the poet tell us: "The sensual and the dark rebel in vain, slaves of their own compulsion." And of all the personal possessions which man can attain on this earth, the most precious is the one of a sound mind controlling a sound body. I close this book by quoting some verses written by Sir Henry Wotton three hundred years ago, which I have all my life considered one of the noblest pieces of poetry in our heritage:

THE CHARACTER OF A HAPPY LIFE

How happy is he born and taught
   That serveth not another's will;
Whose armour is his honest thought
   And simple truth his utmost skill!

Whose passions not his masters are,
  Whose soul is still prepared for death,
Not tied unto the world with care
  Of public fame, or private breath.

Who envies none that chance doth raise
  Or vice; who never understood
How deepest wounds are given by praise;
  Nor rules of state, but rules of good:

Who hath his life from rumours freed,
  Whose conscience is his strong retreat;
Whose state can neither flatterers feed,
  Nor ruin make accusers great:
Who God doth late and early pray
  More of His grace than gifts to lend;
And entertains the harmless day
  With a well-chosen book or friend;

—This man is freed from servile bands
  Of hope to rise, or fear to fall;
Lord of himself, though not of lands;
  And having nothing, yet hath all.

Milton Keynes UK
Ingram Content Group UK Ltd.
UKHW050629270524
443037UK00018B/448